Households
of God
on China's soil

Households
of God
on China's soil

Compiled and translated
by Raymond Fung

ORBIS BOOKS
Maryknoll, New York 10545

The Catholic Foreign Mission Society of America (Maryknoll) recruits and trains people for overseas missionary service. Through Orbis Books Maryknoll aims to foster the international dialogue that is essential to mission. The books published, however, reflect the opinions of their authors and are not meant to represent the official position of the society.

Copyright © 1982 by World Council of Churches, 150 route de Ferney, 1211 Geneva 20, Switzerland; WCC Mission Series No. 2

U.S. edition 1983 by Orbis Books, Maryknoll, NY 10545

All rights reserved

Library of Congress Cataloging in Publication Data

Main entry under title:

Households of God on China's soil.

   Reprint. Originally published: Geneva: World Council of Churches, 1982. (WCC mission series; no. 2)
   Translated from Chinese.
   1. Protestant churches—China—History—20th century. 2. Protestant churches—China—Case studies. 3. China—Church history—20th century. I. Fung, Raymond. II. Series: WCC mission series; no. 2.
BR1288.H68   1983   280'.4'0951   82-18974
ISBN 0-88344-189-6 (pbk.)

CONTENTS

Foreword vii

Preface ix

1. With and without a cross 1

2. A congregation of the Production Brigade 7

3. Arguing and caring 12

4. The East Treasure Jesus Lord Fellowship 18

5. On the campus 24

6. "Your God is a good God" 29

7. The church at home and the church on a hill 35

8. Loving God and loving people 40

9. A Christian village 49

10. Three Bibles and five sets of hymn sheets 54

11. Christian nurture is what we need 59

12. Set apart 64

13. When can we have a Christian "Long March"? .. 69

14. When Jesus did not come again 74

Appendix:
An Open Letter to Brothers and Sisters in Christ of All China from the Standing Committee of the Christian Movement for Self-Government, Self-Support, and Self-Propagation 79

FOREWORD

The churches in China are receiving a good deal of international attention today.

Tourists, church leaders and former missionaries go on frequent visits to China, and they see something of the reality of China as a nation and signs of the presence of the church within that reality. Chinese Christian delegations have also started visiting other countries.

For years we have had no such contacts. We enter this new period of mutual encounter with great hopes and many fears. Hopes, because we can learn so much from the experience of fellow Christians in China. Fears, because we run the risk of bringing our own value judgments to bear on the Chinese situation, and of assuming, with a return to old paternalism, to speak for them.

There is no such danger as far as this book is concerned. Here we let the Chinese Christians speak for themselves. They tell their own stories of churches and Christian people. The stories are not success stories. They do not provide models which can be copied elsewhere. They are of course Christian stories, but they come from a situation which was in many ways unique. They describe how small Christian communities, through one of the most radical upheavals in human history, kept their faith in Jesus Christ — and how their faith kept them. Through services of worship and sessions of Bible study, through caring for people and participating in the nation's life, they witnessed to their faith. Their accounts of how they clung to their faith in times of trial are disarmingly uncomplicated. The strength of their faith and the simple way it is expressed will be an inspiration to Christian people everywhere.

Personally I found these stories deeply moving. They meant a lot to me in my own commitment to Jesus Christ and his church.

We are thankful to our friends in Hong Kong who collected these stories and translated them sensitively into English. We are particularly grateful to our colleague in CWME, Raymund Fung, who introduces the stories and is mainly responsible for their appearance in this form.

>Emilio Castro
>Director, Commission
>on World Mission and Evangelism
>World Council of Churches

PREFACE

Here are 14 stories of Christian communities in the People's Republic of China. They are told by Chinese Christians involved in the life of the communities they describe. Thus they present first-hand experiences of Christian people in China who, after the closure of church buildings, have been meeting for years in homes and other private places for prayer and worship.

A good deal of the material included here was contained in personal letters from Chinese Christians to their friends and relatives in Hong Kong. Additional material was collected through visits to China.

In February 1980, 14 persons came together in Hong Kong to compare notes on evangelization among factory workers. I was one of them. In our conversations China figured frequently. At some point it suddenly came home to us that we had among us considerable information on the church in China. Fragmented but nevertheless reliable information on 19 "house churches" scattered in seven provinces. As we shared what we knew, we hungered for more. Thus was born a commitment to learn about these "house churches" in a more systematic way and to tell their story.

To help us on this journey of learning, each one of us agreed to search for more personal contacts, to seek to fill the gaps in the body of information we already possessed, and to participate in at least one house church meeting. Collectively, we drew up a list of questions to which we wanted answers, in order to learn more about the background of the leader and the beginnings of the group, its practice of worship, its attitude towards the Three-Self Patriotic Movement, its sociological environment and theological expressions. We promised ourselves that we would respect the integrity of the Christians and groups who would open their doors to us.

By October 1980, our pilgrimage had taken us to encounters with forty-two grassroots Christian communities in China, spread over eleven provinces. "Grassroots Christian communities" and not "home churches" — the term we had started with — because by that time available data pointed in that direction.

At one point in our assessment, we contemplated the possibility of extracting the key characteristics from the body of material and attempting a general description. But the size and scope of the samples and their geographical spread were too limited. We discovered, for instance, that one of the 42 cases we studied considers itself to be part of a huge fellowship of some 400 Christian communities in three southern provinces. Since we began assessing our data, more news of grassroots Christian communities along the northern border and among inland minority peoples trickled through.

Of the 42 Christian communities on which we have information 14 have been selected for publication*. We wanted to avoid publishing stories which told of too similar experiences; we wished to eliminate material we were not fully sure of.

What have we learned about the Christian church in China through this encounter?

Perhaps the single most obvious conclusion about Christianity in China today is that it is Chinese. People in the streets and in the communes no longer see Christianity in China as a foreign religion. It was not so before, for reasons we are all familiar with. Big-name converts like Sun Yat Sen and Chiang Kai-sek had not dispelled the general view of Christianity as a foreign faith. Now after some 25 years of isolation, and eight years of acute suffering, with zero visibility, the church is seen to have survived and grown. For the first time in its history, the church has now won its right to exist in China as a Chinese church. For the first time in its existence, it has its roots in Chinese soil. We are convinced that the large body of information on the subject, not only this modest contribution, bears out this conclusion. And, what is equally important, this is how the Chinese people look at Christianity today.

---

* Five of these stories (1, 2, 3, 10 and 14) appeared in the April 1981 issue of the *International Review of Mission*.

That is not to say that the Christian faith is finding a unique Chinese expression. In fact there is little evidence of indigenization in the areas of worship and witness. But there is ample evidence that a daily dialogue goes on between the faith they profess and the struggle in which people are inevitably involved.

Secondly, what Chinese Christians are telling us about themselves is simply this: "We exist, and by the grace of God, we will do the Lord's work in China." As regards the mode or structure of that existence, or the theological emphasis or spiritual texture of that engagement, there is as yet no clear indication. We do not know what kind of church the Christian church in China is going to be like. We have little idea where it is heading. All that we know is that the church in China exists, and exists with vigour and determination.

There is no need to romanticize the Christians in China. Many have kept their faith and continued to bear witness; many have dropped out. Many grassroots Christian communities are fellowships in joy and in suffering; but their life is not free from quarrels and jealousy. There are many whose faith is authentic and whose experience is challenging; there are some whose understanding can only be considered superstitious.

That the central reality of the church in China today is the fact of its existence also means that no one outside can claim proprietorship over it. Confessional and denominational claims have lost their binding power in China. The factors that divide Protestant churches elsewhere have little significance. In this sense, we can speak legitimately of the *Church in China*.

In our experience of the grassroots Christian communities in China, we encountered different traditions and we were exposed to a measure of tension between them. But nowhere have we discovered the kinds of division that lend support to the theory that there are two Protestant churches in China, the "Three-Self church" and the "house church". This leads to our third observation.

Of the 14 grassroots communities included in this book, one is clearly hostile to the Three-Self Movement. The others are either indifferent or positive in their response.

This challenges us to face the question: "Who speaks for the Christian church in China?"

We heard the voices of Christian communities meeting for years in homes or other private places when it was not possible for them to meet publicly as a church. We also heard directly and personally from church leaders in China, and we read and re-read their sermons and statements. We are persuaded that it is one voice. Not that they share the same style of spiritualities. Not that every single Christian in these grassroots communities wishes to join the Three-Self Movement. A few have reservations about some in the leadership. But that they are one in believing and in living out their patriotism, and the principles of self-government, self-support, self-propagation, we have little doubt.

Today, Christians in China are making one declaration to the international Christian communities: "We exist." Existence is grace and is awesome.

This same declaration of existence also requires much of the church in China itself. Existence, awesome as it is, is not enough. There must be content and direction. A church must stand for something. Not so much for the sake of identifying itself with other churches, but for the sake of life, growth and mission. Here, Christians throughout the world wait with expectation. What kind of a church will the church in China be?

Part of the answer, there is little doubt, comes from the fact that the church in China has suffered, and suffered long. Through suffering, the church has found its roots in Chinese soil. Through suffering, it has survived and, with all its diversity, has become truly one. But so far there has not been much of an attempt, as far as we are aware of, on the part of the church in China to reflect on its suffering; nor is there much reflection on its mission amidst the sufferings and struggles of the Chinese people.

Meanwhile, the good news is that the church in China exists and is the church *in China*. This calls for rejoicing. It also calls for respect. Only on the basis of such respect we shall hear what it wishes to tell us.

Raymond W.M. Fung

1. WITH AND WITHOUT A CROSS

The cross has been the centre of our lives and of our meetings. This wooden cross, hand-carved for us by a kind young man, is our fifth, as far as I can remember. You see, we always begin our meetings, as in the old days, with the cross coming into our midst. This way, we feel the heavenly Father with us. One of us would bring in the cross, place it on this stool, and then we would bow. We used to kneel. But we are too old for that now. On occasions, some of us would kneel when we feel particularly weak spiritually. But this often embarrasses others who are only bowing. So we agreed not to kneel. Comrade cadre advised us not to kneel. He said bending one's knees is superstitious. Bowing, however, is more part of religion. Everyone has a right to religion. But superstition should be eliminated. I don't think he knows much about spiritual things. But he's all right. Anyway, we agreed not to kneel. But this sort of thing can't be controlled, you know. It happens. When the cross comes in, and your heart is ready, many thoughts flow over inside.

Yes, this wooden cross, I think, is our fifth. The first was silver, my family's cross. It was one of a set of four. I gave one to each of my three children as a patriotic donation towards the movement to resist the Americans and help the Koreans. All children gave something through their schools. That was in the mid-fifties. I figured this gesture was better than giving cash.

I kept the fourth cross at home. It came in very useful when, towards the end of the fifties, Pastor Pi lost his church and asked my husband if he and others could use our home for prayers. That was how this home meeting began. In the beginning, Pastor Pi used the same big cross, chalice and other sacred things from the church. But to avoid rumour and to show that we Christians were above reproach, he decided not to remove them from the church.

You see, people, even some Christians in the congregation, had begun whispering about him, that he was appropriating church property for his own use. This was bad. So he used my silver cross instead. He told us it was small and meaningful. Probably St Paul had a small silver cross.

For three years, Pastor Pi conducted worship services each Thursday afternoon in this room. I understand he held similar services in two other Christian homes on different days. With him, the cross was always the centre. In my case, we began with about fourteen people, all housewives like me, all members of the congregation. Soon, things became difficult: several had to take regular street patrol duties; others were assigned work hours in canteens and workshops. What with the twice weekly study class, there was not much time. So attendance dropped to an average of three or four. At some time during this period, the silver cross was stolen. It upset Pastor Pi very much. After that, he did not preach any more in the service although I was able to locate another cross, an ivory one. We urged him to go on explaining the word of God to us. He said he was too old and too tired. "Let's just read the word of God and let it speak to us. And the hymns too." So we did, until he died in 1963. Yes, I remember, it was 1963. A good soldier of Christ. Of course I know why he would not preach. He was afraid of one of us mishearing him and informing on him for preaching pessimism. His two fellow pastors who had been living with him in a room in the old church obtained permission for a Christian burial. Members of his family, who had been scattered, were not at the burial, except for his youngest daughter. One of the Christian workers gave a short sermon from, I think, Psalm 73, on the blood of the Christian being precious in the eyes of Jehovah. I learned that a comrade cadre later sought him out for the full text and that they had a good discussion on whether Christian thinking regarded as precious the lives of the revolutionary proletariat. But apparently some Christian house meetings in the town had problems, because three groups split on this score. Our group, however, continued. We met around the ivory cross. We prayed. We read the word of God. We prayed some more. Then we sang familiar hymns and read the unfamiliar ones. The hours passed quietly.

The early sixties were difficult times. Everything was short. Outside the hours of sleep, everyone was supposed to keep on working, except that there wasn't that much work available, especially for old people like us. But we could not remain idle. So we took to queuing on meat lines and movie-ticket lines, for ourselves and for our neighbours. It was the best way in the circumstances to talk or to be left alone. If you are on the food line you are never interfered with.

Our Thursday afternoon meeting continued; I was practically the leader. We were four. To save fuel, our families came together for supper, with every one bringing his or her own rice and fish. Sometimes we prayed too long, and when we opened our eyes, we could see our grown-up sons and daughters and their children quietly praying too. Then there were over twenty of us. After prayers I took the cross away, and we began to prepare our meal. But news spread of our pooling our food for a common meal on these occasions. One day we found five other families joining in the meeting. Of course they did not come for the prayers. They came for the common meal. They each had a small portion of rice with them, but they ate a disproportionate lot. We couldn't say no. We kept our smiles. But somehow, they never came back for a second time. Maybe they felt ashamed.

Then the Cultural Revolution came upon us. Almost overnight, pavements, verandah supports, walls were painted with big character slogans and the single word "loyalty". Rumours of all sorts filled the air. There were physical clashes in the streets. Red guards rode in open trucks singing and shouting. We stopped our Thursday meetings.

One day, my neighbour's 14-15 year-old son with two friends wearing the Red Guard 132 armbands came to my door and quietly tipped me off about "a house confiscation" visit by Red Guards any time. I was so frightened I cried on the spot. The youngsters comforted me, told me it was routine, and that I should get rid of my Jesus things, although, they hastened to add, "everyone on the block knows you are a Jesus believer". I prayed all night. My husband, who had never joined me in the meetings, also broke down and prayed. He told me to get rid of the ivory cross. So I hid it in the charcoal pile in the kitchen. Three days later they arrived, over forty of them, most standing outside, bearing small placards on which was painted a single character "loyalty". The leaders were nervous, but tried to be cool and firm. They announced their purpose was to eliminate the four "olds", but not "old mamas". They bowed in front of my Mao poster and searched the place. They found my ivory cross with ease. The leader took it right in front of me, moved his young head in mock pity, let the cross fall and crushed it with his foot. I was too scared to react. So went my second cross. My Bibles and hymns and several other books were also confiscated. The leaders left. Then the others came in and took away all my valuables and furniture, leaving only two chairs and a table, saying: "You have too much, others have none." Several days later, two families moved into my house. One occupied the now empty second bedroom, and the other placed themselves in the corridor.

With strangers in the house and the threat of the Cultural Revolution, we held no more Thursday meetings. All eight Christian groups in the area ceased to function. At the start, the two Christian workers living in the old church paid regular visits. But when one was paraded in the street as a "cow", the visits stopped. I never saw them again.

Public worship has been reintroduced since early 1980. We got word from our friends, and one of the three pastors paid us a visit during our Thursday meetings. We urged him to preach to us. It had been so long since we last heard a sermon. He said he wasn't prepared. He's getting old and, like us, had not heard a sermon for a long time. He held the cross for us. And he cried. Finally, he informed us of the opening of the church, invited us to take part, encouraged us to remain steadfast in the Lord.

Later the nine of us talked about the re-opened church nearby. It wasn't the church I was baptized in. But no matter. Finally everyone agreed that the next Sunday I should go and take a look. There was apparently some hesitation on the part of the younger people, because they had heard that people had to be registered as Christian before being allowed in. I was too old to worry. So I went early; there was no registration. A church worker told me that there had been thoughts of building up a membership roll. She said a worship service is no church. A church is a family of Christians witnessing, serving and of course worshipping together. Hence the idea of getting worshippers to sign their names and addresses. But the idea was dropped as premature. People were suspicious, with reason. So I went to church. It was heavenly. My heart was full of blessings and my eyes full of happy tears. I shamelessly clutched the arm of an old man sitting next to me, wetting his jacket with my tears. I was so happy I had a headache. My heart beat fast every time the congregation sang and the piano played. It was too much for me. Now I can only remember the sermon title. It was "Jesus the Shepherd". That's why I have never gone back again. Comrade doctor said I got excited too easily. So now the young people went, and then in our Thursday meetings, they told us the sermon they heard in church. Two did very well. I hope they can one day become preachers.

Then I decided to make a small cross for myself. I put two short branches together, wrapped them with a piece of woollen cloth and sewed them up. It looked really nice and the size fits my palm. I carried it all the time in my pocket, touching it and remembering Jesus.

Then my son and his wife came back and lived with us. Both are physicians in Peking. They must have suffered greatly. They would not let me know the details. They had lost their jobs, their home and their belongings. And I had nothing to give them. One evening when we gathered for supper, I took my courage in both hands and told my husband, my son and my daughter-in-law that we used to say grace at meal time and that I would like to pray for them. Without waiting for their response, I took out my cross, put it at the middle of the table and said the Lord's Prayer. I heard my son joining me in broken phrases. He remembered portions of it from his Sunday school days. From that day on, we said grace before every meal, and occasionally prayed for my daughter and her husband who are in Hupei. It was a far cry from the two- to three-hour prayer meeting we had had before the Cultural Revolution. But I am sure it must have been equally pleasing in the eyes of the heavenly Father. I gave my cross to my daughter-in-law and made another one for myself. She is a very intelligent woman. I hope the cross will help her.

In 1978, our Thursday meetings somehow got going again. Two of my Christian friends turned up and we began all over again. Things were more relaxed then. My son and his wife returned to Peking, having got back their jobs and their home. The Cheng family, one of the two living in the same house, have joined us in prayer. So now we are ten, sometimes twelve, fourteen. It's too crowded. Maybe when the other family move out — they have to, you know, under the new arrangement — we could have more room.

There is hope in my heart. There are now over forty of us in our Thursday meetings. We have six Bibles. I've got back most of my furniture so the older people can sit on benches. And we've got a bigger cross, hand-carved by one of our young people. Since he's one of our "imitation" preachers, we let him bring in the cross. We all have had difficult times. But our heavenly Father has been good to us.

2. A CONGREGATION OF THE PRODUCTION BRIGADE

It took the two of us two full days to go to a proper Christian service in Shanghai. We wanted to see how it's done. There are two hundred and ten of us worshipping Jesus in five places in our commune. We've been doing it for five years on our own. We want to learn more, much more about the Bible, about theology, about Christianity, in Shanghai and in other places.

All of us belong to the same Production Brigade. We know what's going on in Shanghai. So when we learned of a church re-opening for public worship, we were selected to go and find out as much as we could and to see if we could get hold of Bibles, hymnals and other books.

There was no problem getting leave. Finding a place to spend the night in Shanghai was more difficult.

We know about the Three-Self Patriotic Movement, but not very much. There is an old "uncle" among us who used to be a pastor near Shanghai, and he told us that he had signed the Three-Self Declaration in the fifties. We had been thinking of sending him on the Shanghai trip. He was too weak. He encouraged us younger men to go and to use his name to get introduced. Several brothers and sisters, however, suggested that we simply observe the service without making ourselves known to the officials there. We promised to be cautious. This matter came before the business session of our church on the eve of our departure. After discussion, Brother Miu, who is 46 and a leading brother, decided that while we must exercise caution, we should explore ways of getting in touch with other Christians. We all agreed. You see, ours is the only Christian group in the area. The only church building crumbled several years back and all the bricks were taken away. We are also fairly well known in our commune. We have gone through the shadow of the valley of death, we have little to fear. We have nothing to hide.

Organizationally, our congregation conforms to the structure of the Production Brigade. We didn't start this way. We were more or less forced into it. But since most of us have come from two neighbouring villages, it makes sense. It happened when our Brigade decided to respond enthusiastically to the Party's call to grow more wheat. At the time, comrade secretary suggested that we Jesus believers band together as a small unit. At first this move made the other families uneasy, but there's no problem now. Although our conditions were not exactly right for wheat growing, we managed reasonably well, and the others seemed happy to be with us. So here we are, about two hundred of us — the Believers' Team, as others jokingly describe us. Actually, we are only slightly more than one half of the Brigade. Nevertheless, we are entitled to the use of the big meeting hall. We could have used it for worship services each Sunday if we wanted to. But we don't, taking into consideration the feelings of others, especially the youngsters who would undoubtedly flock to the meeting. Some would show a sincere interest. Others would be hostile and might ever jeer. So we stick to meetings at homes, although in every sense we are one unit, one church.

Our church has no money; there's no need. Keeping a full account is troublesome and can cause suspicion. We don't want to be answering questions such as "why the money?" "where does it come from?", etc. from our comrade cadres. Besides, we don't know which department to turn to for accountability. Comrade secretary didn't know. He told us "nobody has heard of a believers' audit". So we keep no accounts and take up no regular offering. Whenever we have needs, we ask brothers and sisters to contribute. The Shanghai trip for the two of us, for instance, we estimated to cost RMB$110 and Brother Miu felt we needed another $100 in case Bibles, books and paper were available. So we announced the need and took a collection. From the five prayer groups, we obtained over $250.

One reason for the good response is the addition to our church of four new families, each of which has four to five adult working hands. They have a lot of work points and so are not tight in their money. Brother Miu baptized them in the stream. We did it quietly because while worshipping

Jesus has become acceptable to the leading comrades, having one's sins washed away by baptism is still regarded by many as superstition. Of course there was no way we could hide it from the Brigade. But there's no reason to start a noisy discussion either. Spiritual things are not understood by the world.

One of the baptized families is the Chang family, consisting of the father and three grown-up sons; the mother had died recently. She was a Christian, a good woman who never stopped working in the field and in the house. She never complained. When she finally collapsed about a year ago, we took time to visit her and to try to take care of her. Her sons were often there also, and joined in the prayer silently. Maybe this experience was what caused their conversion. The Sunday after the funeral, we found the three young men present at one of our house meetings. After the first part, during the meal break — they had their lunch with them — I couldn't help drawing them aside and asking them why they were present. The eldest looked surprised: "We want to be Jesus believers." We praised the Lord and asked them to give their testimonies. But they couldn't say much. They just wanted to be Jesus believers. We got word to Brother Miu who later visited them at their home. Brother Miu later told us they were indeed true believers.

They were baptized at 5 a.m. several Sundays later in the cold stream. Old Pa Chang was there, too, looking on. "You are dead and buried," Brother Miu intoned. The three immersed themselves completely. Then he lifted them up by the chin, and said: "Now you are raised up, your sin is gone." We clapped hands in happiness. Old Pa Chang sitting on the bank also applauded. A hard-working peasant, his wife of many years dead now, he wanted to share in his sons' joy. Big Sister Miu helped him to his feet and asked if he too would become a Jesus believer. He shook his head: "I will not do anything joyful for one year. After one year, maybe." "But Big Sister Chang would have liked to see you become a Jesus believer, and your sons." "Yes, but not for one year, not when my wife has just died." Since then, Old Pa Chang has been a regular participant at our worship, with his sons.

We had our beginning five years back. It was a hard time, a very difficult time. Mass meetings, newspaper-reading sessions to learn the mass line. Youngsters sent from cities making a lot of noise in the open, turning our village upside down. A few, however, seemed to have given up, refusing to go into the fields, just idling around, boys and girls shamelessly fondling each other. Loudspeakers blaring slogans continually. Tension was high. Peasants and students exchanging foul language. Hordes of strangers passing through, sometimes asking for water and food. There was confusion everywhere. Comrade secretary seemed to have disappeared. Nobody knew what was going on.

Then something happened. A young woman who was a Red Guard leader suddenly went crazy. She was visibly pregnant. She had been one of the most dedicated and selfless Red Guards based in our village. She worked with us in the field. She taught us the thoughts of Chairman Mao. She taught songs to the children. She was tough with some local cadres and leading comrades, but she never used foul language. And she never complained. Now we were shocked to see her behave like a mad woman. She cried. She laughed. She sat and lay on the ground. She became filthy. On occasions, she jumped on passers-by and asked people to feel her belly. Her fellow comrades tried to look after her, but she wouldn't let them. Treatment in the clinic didn't work. There was not much medicine available anyway. A few suggested that a demon had crawled into her body. At this point, Brother Miu took her into his home. His whole family looked after her. But she didn't improve.

One day, Grandma Moi came to our village again. She used to be a worker in a small Christian church in the area. The church of course was long gone. So she went around visiting the Christians. There were no Christians in our village, but she came anyway. My father said there must have been some Jesus believers here, but perhaps they no longer believed in religion now. But we all liked Grandma Moi. She was educated and whenever she came, about once or twice every three months, she would give the children some candy that she made at home. She seldom talked about her religion. In normal times, she would stay for two days, having no problem getting permission from the security office. We all welcomed her to our homes. But it became troublesome during the Cultural Revolution. So her visits had been a lot less frequent. But now here she was, a small, alert old woman.

Brother Miu took grandma to his home and told her Lee's story. Lee was the Red Guard who was not right in her head. So grandma tried to talk to Lee and fed her porridge. At night, the two shared the came cotton quilt.

According to Brother Miu, the next morning saw grandma kneeling beside the bunk and praying for Lee. Grandma was so rapt in her prayer that she wasn't aware of anything else. Nobody interrupted her. When Lee woke up, she was a different person. You could see from her eyes that she was no longer crazy. The demon was gone. She was still weak. Grandma stayed for several more days, looking after her. Neighbours sent in food and soup. People gathered outside in wonder.

Some time during these days, Brother Miu and his wife secretly became Jesus believers. They later testified that they saw an angel hovering over grandma as she cared for Lee. I learned that Lee, on her departure, turned over several Bibles and other religious books to Brother Miu, taken apparently from the Red Guard quarters.

After a week or so, Grandma Moi left us, amazingly in the company of Lee's Red Guards. Lee was looking after *her* this time. This was about five years ago. Grandma Moi has come back twice since then to help Brother Miu preach the gospel. Several old Christians have also reappeared. They are very helpful. Brother Miu is our leading brother. He asked me to believe in Jesus, and I said yes. I will believe in Jesus all my life.

Our hope is to build a church, not as big as the one we went to in Shanghai, of course. Something simple but beautiful.

3. ARGUING AND CARING

Even at the worst times, we managed to meet every week for prayer and scripture reading. Like in the 1966-68 period, we persevered by breaking up into groups of three or four, gathering in homes, under a tree in the field, or in the parks, praying with our eyes open and mouths smiling as if we were talking and sharing a joke. We have our hymns and scripture portions developed on palm-sized photographic paper, just like a photograph. You know you unwrap the paper, which is very sensitive to light, in the dark; you put a positive or transparency with words on top of it, sandwich them between two panes of glass and expose it in the sun for two minutes. You get an exact copy, except that you have white words on a black background. It is a bit hard on the eyes for elderly people, but it comes in handy, and it keeps better than ordinary paper. And most important, it is easily duplicated. Up to now, our church has over one hundred different pieces, and enough copies for use in a worship service for about eighty people.

Since 1969, we have been meeting again as a whole group. We have an ideal setting — eight Christian families living in a five-house compound opening up to an inner open court. We meet in one of the houses, utilizing for sitting purposes the house, the covered porch and the open court. In winter, we squeeze all the elderly people inside and the young people pack themselves in the porch.

This way, we keep each other warm. The difficulty is getting down on our knees. We are so crowded sitting on the floor with our knees almost touching our chest that every time we set out to pray, there is an inevitable commotion. Rev. Yeong, whom we regard as our pastor, joked that this was good because it woke up those who were falling asleep. Indeed, I can say there are always a few who do.

At the moment, we have three services, two on Saturday and one on Sunday. This has happened because, since early

1980 when the People's Government announced the normal implementation of the policy of religious freedom guaranteed by the constitution, there have been many more people wanting to come to worship. Quite a few are elderly people who have been Christians all along. Now they wish to be part of us. There are also a number of middle-aged teacher comrades whose reputation, labelled as rightist during the Cultural Revolution, has been restored. They too can come out into the open. The rest are simply curious. This fact has caused us a lot of problems.

In the first place, many of our old folk began to complain that the newcomers didn't pray and didn't take part in the worship in a spiritual manner. Which is true enough. While they followed every step of the service without fail, they would begin using foul language once the blessing was given, even before they stepped out of the house. Several of us, including myself, talked to them and asked them to respect the house of God. They apologized but once they opened their mouth, bad language simply rushed out. There was no stopping it.

The other occurrence has to do with Brother Fong, a teacher in his fifties who recently joined us. A keen Christian, he raised the matter of having services on Sundays. We explained our Seventh Day Adventist practice, and also our desire to work and worship with other Christians. That ended the matter for a short while.

Given the many problems, we decided eventually to have a second service on Saturday at five early in the evening and a Sunday service beginning at twelve noon. Rev. Yeong would continue to lead the original Saturday service. Brother Nga was to lead the early evening session, and Brother Fong and I the one on Sunday. At the moment, all three services are doing fine, although Brother Nga's service has not been as well attended as the other two. Of course when it comes to communion, Rev. Yeong is still the person. He's the only one in holy office.

The issue of communion — who can celebrate it? how should it be done? — is still an unsettled issue. Among the 400 churches in our network in the southeast provinces, there is disagreement about it. The same is true of our group. Some of us feel that only properly ordained persons should break the bread. Others, many others including myself, do not feel this way. We don't see this in the scriptures. And what is more, ordination itself is no less controversial. Rev. Yeong was ordained long before the liberation. He must be eighty now. So he's no problem. But as far as I know, in our region in the last twenty years there have been at least fifty persons ordained, and most, I dare say, serve the Lord very well. However some brothers and sisters in other churches simply would not have them, and would not give them respect. But the old generation of pastors is almost all gone. For our own church here, despite my own feelings and others', we want to defer to Pastor Yeong. We don't want to argue on ordination. For me, the most essential thing is to work with all the Christians like Brother Fong, learn to pray and worship together, and then see if we can find some opportunities to preach the word of God. That's why I want to work with him.

Still, disputes and controversies have plagued us, causing bitterness and anguish among brothers and sisters, at a time when we so much need each other. Perhaps we are simply too big. There are some four hundred of our house groups in the southern provinces alone. Most of us never see each other; the leading brothers do. Each house group is very much on its own. There are, however, a certain number of exchanges of hymns and scripture portions. This is good. In 1963, when food was scarce everywhere in our province, news came to our group that several others, some twenty of our house groups in the next commune, were so short that starvation was likely to occur.

Rev. Yeong told us the news and we naturally began scraping together what we could spare. We were in a slightly better position because our commune had some land patches for tobacco-growing. Finally we got together some eleven bags of dry food, each weighing about thirty kilos. They came and took them away. Before they left, they held our hands and loudly said praises to the Lord. Rev. Yeong said this was New Testament Christianity. We were all very moved.

Our trouble came next Saturday when what we did somehow became known. At the end of the service, comrade cadre and several other officials were waiting at the inner court. They came to the front, and openly accused us, the Jesus people, of food stealing and attempts to sabotage the system of distributing food. Although most of what we had given away was our own, there was a small portion which could be said to belong to the Production Brigade — the dried fish, the black beans and certainly the bags. We were frightened. We tried to explain why we did it. But it didn't get through. There were too many people shouting and cursing. After five or six hours of continuous haranguing, I and two other brothers pleaded guilty on behalf of the group. The three of us had our ration reduced for six months. The whole church also had to pay back the food by instalment. It was very hard on us. This event also soured the relationship between the Christians and others which till then had been normal and carefree. It was later in the "big lessons" (political discussions) that I came to realize the source of the resentment. In their eyes, the over-riding fact was that we had shown more concern for the Christians in the neighbouring commune than for fellow villagers in the same commune. Indeed, we had taken food away from one commune and given it to our friends in the other. They of course have a point. But we had failed to see it. This experience caused us much physical hardship. But it has also taught us a deep lesson — that Christians must learn to be open to people. We must learn to love as Jesus loved. We came to see the whole picture. I think this perspective has helped us since then.

The bad thing about being part of a 400 group fellowship is that we have many hearts and wills. As I said earlier, there are among us, inevitably, differences of opinion on baptism, communion, ordination and a whole lot of other church things. The key question is who. Who can do what? When I was young in the pre-Liberation days, these questions were not serious. We followed the Americans. But now the headquarters is no more. The old pastors have almost died out. Younger men like me are ministering. The people in our own group trust us. But others don't necessarily. They say some of us are not ordained in the proper way. That we are allowing non-Adventist people to dilute our faith and so forth. Lately, there has been an even more serious row. Since the change of national policy in

1979, several of our leaders and pastors have had their reputations restored, along with their accumulated wages and their homes. But some, for whatever reasons, have not been so lucky. Now this does not appear on the surface to have anything to do with the church, but it does. Because unless you are restored, and become a citizen in good standing, you have no standing among people and with the cadres. This is crucial at a time when there is a chance to repossess church premises presently used for other purposes.

Nevertheless, I believe we are going in the right direction. When the Three-Self Patriotic Movement officials asked us to take part in the running of public services in two newly-repossessed churches, we responded positively. Now, two of our pastors are in team ministry with others from other backgrounds, working together, worshipping together. There is no more Adventist Church. There is the Adventist tradition. But it is one church. When we first got the invitation, some of us were fairly apprehensive. Memories die hard. But as we began seeking the view of the home groups, it was obvious that most were in favour of working with the Three-Self Patriotic Movement. Practically speaking, we are already holding public worship and hymn singing. I don't think we could have come to this understanding had it not been for what we and all the other Christians went through in the past twenty years.

So this is our story. We are still worshipping in the homes. There are no church premises around in suitable condition. The only one left standing has no roof and it's some six kilometres away. I don't see the possibility of erecting a new church. There are no laws, no regulations, no permission. So perhaps we'll just build and worry later. But wood is extremely difficult to come by. And besides, what will others say — I mean those who want wood to build houses for their sons to get married in? But once in a while, it is good to go into town and worship in a real church.

Our meetings began a long while ago, even before the liberation. At that time, we had a sort of minority complex in relation to other Christians. So we had a strong tradition of family teaching, of learning about our faith at home. My local church, for instance, had divided up the congregation into five family groups for weekly gatherings for prayer, instruction and lessons about health. And then we had farsighted leaders who kept on emphasizing the home. I remember, several months before the closing of our church premises, we were already urged to memorize Psalms 90, 94, 103, 119, 121, and 139. That was how we began. During the Cultural Revolution, very few of us dared to meet regularly, certainly not with thirty to forty people. We broke into threes or fours. In the circumstances, we couldn't sing, we couldn't have a sermon. What most of us did was simply recite the psalms, or make new ones. When you are close to God, God will move your lips. Here's one a sister made, probably after Psalm 121:

> The eyes of the merciful Lord are upon me,
> For my mind's eyes can see so clearly.
> No dark clouds separate us.
>
> Let enemies come and blindfold me,
> Or burn my sight with painful torches.
> The all-seeing Lord will protect me,
> Lending me his unfailing sight.
>
> Slumber not, my caring Lord,
> Sleep not, the Merciful.
> Do not turn your face away,
> Though my look be so ungainly
> And my body frail.
>
> Rejoice, for the Lord sees me,
> His sight kindly restores me,
> Now and on Resurrection Day.

4. THE EAST TREASURE JESUS LORD FELLOWSHIP

I am a medical worker. I became a Jesus believer in 1970 and a member of a church of some three hundred people in a production brigade.

As a medical worker in a municipal hospital, I and other doctors had to take turns to go to the countryside to serve the peasants. It was hard work; travelling long distances in a worn-out jeep, eating food with flies all over it. On one occasion, I was served what looked like a tiny fish cooked with a generous supply of black soy bean. It was indeed a tiny fish, but with a thousand flies, live flies, with their jaws in my supper. I tried to wave them away. But it was useless; they kept coming back. I had to grind my teeth and proceed to eat the fish as if the flies weren't there. It was a real struggle. Those were the kinds of conditions we medical workers had to endure. Naturally, most of us in the hospital were reluctant to go, especially those with a wife and children. A normal three-day round was like a three-month ordeal. I was single. So I volunteered to stand in for my older colleagues. Soon I was spending more than half my days in the rural areas. Life was very hard out there. People had need of medical care. I was not unhappy. It turned out to be my salvation, in two senses of the word.

When the Radical Pioneering Fellowship, a militant Red Guard organization, took over the municipal hall in late 1966, I was some 300 kilometres away from the city, showing a film on fever treatment from village to village and treating patients. Soon, bits and pieces of news filtered through. All my doctor colleagues were put on a half-day work schedule, with the other half given over to reflection and writing, first on the hospital administration, and secondly on their own performance as Marxist-Leninist medical workers. Four days later, I learned that they were not allowed to go home, but had to go on with their reflection into late hours. I was summoned to return. It was a verbal message, conveyed to me by one of the leading cadres in the production brigade.

My heart was very heavy as I packed my gear. I didn't know what to do. I was afraid. It was then that Comrade To entered my life. A stocky man in his fifties, he was one of the people's leaders, always present in commune meetings. But he was not an official leader. Secretaries and leading cadres seldom addressed questions to him. They must have considered him strange and unpredictable. Anyway, I was visibly shaking while I packed my projector and charts and other gear, when Comrade To walked into the meeting hall, came over to my corner, and said to me: "I think you should stay. We will take care of you." I broke down like a child. "Can I?"

I spent the night in the guest room, while about thirty brigade sub-unit leaders met informally with the secretary and his two associate cadres to talk about my case. I was later to learn that not much happened in the meeting. Everyone was sympathetic, including the Partymen, some more, some less. But only a handful, including Comrade To, had strong feelings about keeping me. Anyway, very early next morning, Comrade To and several of his neighbours took me to their village. They asked me to sign over my gear to the workshop and take only my personal belongings with me. So I was taken in by a neighbour of Comrade To, Tien Big Uncle, a widower. He told me he was almost seventy, he had nothing to fear, and that Jesus Lord would protect us.

This was my first inkling of religion coming straight at me. There was to be much more. Thus began the first day of my eight-year stay with Tien Big Uncle, right in the midst of a church known by its members and neighbours as the East Treasure Jesus Lord Fellowship. That same evening, Tien took me over to Comrade To's place. Over twenty people sat, knelt or stood, praying out loud. I couldn't understand what was being said, except that I could hear my name mentioned occasionally. I was scared. When I closed my eyes, I felt better.

The praise-giving meeting turned out to be a nightly affair, lasting some two hours, with people freely coming and leaving. Most of the time, people just closed their eyes and simply spoke. Then someone would shout "Amen", others would follow with their series of "Amen" with decreasing sound volume until there was silence. It was then time for someone to address the group. On this occasion Comrade To spoke about me, he said that Jesus Lord had committed me to their keeping. While I was not a Jesus believer, he knew in his heart that I would soon become one because Jesus' Spirit had been working in me, as was proved by the fact that I had chosen to leave the city hospital to work in the countryside. That wasn't quite true. But I was deeply moved. Then the praises began again. Two elderly women held me in their arms as they prayed. I soon found myself repeating after them over and over again "Jesus Lord", "Jesus Lord", "Jesus Lord".

Sunday late afternoon was worship time. Over three hundred people, old and young, gathered in a barn and its courtyard which used to be a school. Comrade To, his wife and three middle-aged people were in charge. They stood straight, facing the people, and spoke in unison: "In the name of the Jesus Lord, we command ghosts, demons and forces of darkness to depart from this place." Then Comrade To's wife, To Big Aunt, led us in singing very simple homemade tunes to the words of Jesus Lord's parables, repeating over and over again: "Ploughing the field deep and rich, aiah, aiah. A treasure hidden there deep and rich, aiah, aiah. Jesus is my Treasure Lord, aiah, aiah. Out in the field, in the field." And in all, I counted some twenty such songs during my stay. Reflecting on my experience of being a Jesus believer, I must say these songs have provided me with a light-heartedness and sense of ease in understanding and being which I could not find in other areas of life in China these many years. After the songs, the demonstration word (sermon). It consisted, without fail, in reading long passages of the Bible, lasting some 30-45 minutes. Then Comrade To and other leaders who had Bibles would talk about a verse here and a verse there, always urging us to listen to the command of Jesus Lord. Sometimes, they read in unison, other times responsively. On several occasions, they would invite young people in senior high school to read the scriptures. It was considered a great honour, and a lot of work was always put in beforehand to prepare the young people, as they had so little experience with the Bible, and the printed characters were of the old type. Even so, at the public reading, they always managed to make mistakes and, when corrected by To Big Aunt, would make everybody laugh. Finally came Bible recitation time. Every Sunday, we were supposed to learn a few verses by heart. It was always fun. The old women provided most of it. They giggled. They shouted loudly to have the verse repeated over and over again. They messed things up. They jeered at people who failed to do it right and wildly applauded those who did. At one point, Comrade To was so angry he openly scolded the old women. He warned them not to take the word of the heavenly Father lightly. There was dead silence. His wife had to break the routine and get the people to start singing again in order to wind up the worship.

The incident led to a discussion among the leaders on whether we should abandon the practice. Comrade To insisted that with less than ten Bibles in the whole church, the practice must continue. He won. We continued to memorize a verse or two every Sunday, and the old women continued to have fun.

The mainstay of the church remained the nightly praise-giving meeting where people prayed aloud. Occasionally, sick people were brought in to be embraced and, it was hoped, healed. Brother To seldom laid hands on the sick, but Brother Sit and his wife were much more adept at it. I was once asked by Brother To what I, as a doctor, felt about healing by prayer. I turned away from discussing the subject, not knowing much about it, and being aware that it was a subject too sensitive for a guest to talk about, although I was now practically part of the fellowship. It was common knowledge that Brother Sit made a living out of visiting the sick and laying hands on them. Brother To was most unhappy about it. An open confrontation at a church business meeting did not resolve the issue. Brother To's criticism was that a Jesus believer should not use prayer for money, and that the reputation of the East Treasure Jesus Lord Fellowship would suffer. Brother Sit explained that he never asked for payment. People gave to show their appreciation, and anyway he had always turned part of the money over to the church.

At one point, I was asked by the church to find out if Brother Sit could indeed cure the sick by prayer. To my surprise, Brother Sit raised no objection, and in fact welcomed my presence. So I went out with him occasionally. Brother Sit would introduce me as a doctor, and ask me to help examine the sick and to explain the illness to the family. Then he would lay his hand on the sick spot and pray aloud, sometimes asking relatives to join in. After this, we would leave. It was never possible to find out if any cure had occurred. Soon I began to suspect that Brother Sit was making use of me. I was asked to accompany him on his visits more frequently. I grew uneasy, and finally stopped going altogether.

Looking back, I suppose this experience was one of the reasons I did not become a Jesus believer until 1970. I had no problem during the praise-giving meetings. I truly believed. But afterwards I wasn't sure. By 1970, I felt I had to take a stand. One Sunday, I told my story at the worship service. I said how Jesus Lord had saved me both physically and spiritually, and that I pledged to serve him the rest of my life. Brother To, Brother Sit and others immediately declared me a Jesus believer. I now had a family of many many Jesus believers.

According to Brother To, the East Treasure Jesus Lord Fellowship had its origin in some twenty members from three congregations: Baptist, Presbyterian and Meeting Hall (Little Flock). In the fifties, the three began meeting as one congregation (except for communion). Membership dwindled; only about twenty remained. By 1962, all the ordained and lay leaders were gone, with their Bibles and hymnals. Only a handful of Jesus believers were left. Brother To, a self-educated farmer who had hitherto been content to let others run the church, gradually emerged as the leader. As a sub-unit captain in the production brigade, he was beyond suspicion. Christians, some of whom he had never known before, began to come back in around him. It was said by others that Brother To had had a number of encounters with Jesus Lord. But he would not speak of these. He was a man of few words, except when he prayed in the praise-giving meeting.

I had my own work assignment during these years. I teamed up with Tien Big Uncle in caring for the fruit trees. I attended to the medical needs of the villagers. I also wrote out golden verses in large simplified characters to help the old women memorize the Bible. Life was hard. But I was grateful. At the height of the Cultural Revolution, over four hundred Red Guards were in official control of our commune. They ordered us to yield up all poisonous literature. We complied, not wanting them to come into our village. So our few Bibles disappeared. But when they enquired about me, Brother To exercised his influence and simply ignored the enquiry. Other villages did likewise. But everybody was worried. Brother To and Tien Big Uncle not least. We cut our Sunday meeting time to half, meeting in two separate groups inside the barn. We had only a weekly praise-giving meeting, with some of us posted as guards. When I left the immediate neighbourhood to attend to the sick, Brother To had four of his friends keep me company to prevent me from being taken away by the Red Guards. I was able to teach them basic first aid and how to collect herbs for medicine.

By 1975, I received a letter from my mother that I could come home. Things were clearing up. Tien Big Uncle threw a party for some twenty friends, including of course Brother To. He advised us not to publicize the news of my departure. He didn't want the young people to have ideas. We prayed, and I asked him to lay his hand on my head. He wouldn't. Instead he asked me solemnly to find out how I could serve the East Treasure Jesus Lord Fellowship when I got back to the city: "You know our needs. See what you can do." Then we went to the workshop to claim back my gear. The projector was gone, the charts were torn. I vowed in my heart to come back with a new projector, new film and new charts.

5. ON THE CAMPUS

Yes, we regard our meetings at home as a local church in spiritual fellowship with the worldwide Christian community. We began as a prayer group for Christian students at the university about 1952 when it had become untenable to have our meetings on campus ground. There was no rule against our continuing to use the physics laboratory in my department. But to avoid making it difficult for myself and my chancellor, who was a friend of my father and who had increasingly to work with party appointees most of whom had very little understanding of Christianity, the students and I decided to meet at my home. At first, we met in the spacious house of a student leader whose parents owned a number of textile mills. But we soon realized it was a stupid thing to do, risky for them and for everybody. So after two sessions, we moved to my quarters. It was amazing how sensitive one became in the exciting but fragile environment at the beginning of the People's China. Actually we had hoped to locate the prayer group in a students' dormitory. But it was not to be. They didn't allow women in the evenings. So we met in my quarters in the professors' compound at four every Wednesday afternoon. We did the things we had always done in varsity fellowship — singing, Bible studies, intercession, fellowship, but with, I believed, more depth and more openness. I was moved by the rapid spiritual growth of the young people. Nobody knew what to expect exactly. More than ever we had to learn to depend on God.

As a teacher of physics, I must confess my political level was then very low. I love teaching physics. I love students. As long as I was allowed to do that, I was a happy man, or so I thought. This attitude was seriously challenged by the leading political cadre who came to our departmental meeting one day. His opening statement was straightforward: "In Socialist China, the supreme function of the teacher is to propagate Marxist-Leninism to the next generation." He then went on to other household chores. At the time, I was secretly relieved he didn't go on. How was I, a Christian lecturer, to propagate Marxist-Leninism? Luckily he didn't pursue the subject. But the question has stayed with me.

Not so much in that formulation, but in a more general way concerning the Christian gospel and China's standing up on her own two feet. Much later in 1967, two years into the Cultural Revolution, the question came to me again, sharp as an arrow. Together with two other Christian colleagues, we were called into the Red Guard base on the campus. They asked us: "How can religious-superstitious right-roaders propagate Marxist-Leninism and Mao T'se tung Thought?" We had been advised beforehand not to engage in self-defence as it would be fruitless and only prolong the humiliation. So we bowed our heads in silence and accepted the dismissal. My mind was numb. They had taken away the only thing I care about in life. As a right-roader, I had little rights. I lost my job. I lost my quarters. And I lost my life with students.

But this did not happen until 1967. Between 1952 and 1964, the prayer group had its ups and downs. We had never more than some thirty or so students. During the most difficult times in 1962, there were only my wife and me. But the important thing was that God had left a Christian witness on campus during these years.

We had a lot of problems, mostly from within. Although we never made any public announcement of our meeting, it was a known fact on the campus, and often new people came. I mean Christian students who had not been with us before. And soon we were faced with the same problems that the churches were facing in society. At the time, the missionaries were leaving. It was a natural thing to pray for the ones we knew, praying for their safety on the return trip, and praising God for their faithfulness. But some students were hostile to the missionaries. They prayed that God would forgive them, and also forgive the American churches who had sold the gospel of Jesus Christ to the highest capitalistic bidder. It came to a point where we could not pray and have fellowship as a group. The atmosphere was so tense one could feel it. I personally did not doubt their sincerity but I was angry that they brought politics into prayer. Politics kept us from an awareness of the presence of God. The leadership met over the weekend, prayed and fasted and finally decided to clean up our own house. A confrontation took place in a special session. It lasted the whole night.

I don't think we handled it very well. There were things we could not say out loud but which were basic to our alienation from each other. Everyone knew it. It was that kind of situation. Finally, Kuo, the fellowship's chairman, pushed through the use of the traditional seven-point doctrinal test. Those who endorsed wholeheartedly orthodox Christianity as expressed in the seven points — like the virgin birth, etc. — stayed. Those who would not subscribe to them had to leave.

It was a sad day when this happened. I guess it had to be done. But what shocked everybody was the decision of our devotional leader whose evangelical conviction and love for the Lord were totally unquestionable. He decided to leave us for one year. He had no problem with the doctrinal matters. But he could not accept what we had done. He said he needed to be involved much more with what was going on in China. He said he would return in a year. He never did.

It was our first split. It reduced the number to around twenty. The second split came soon after. Some who stayed wanted the group to become a church. Some in the group didn't want to return to their local churches which were undergoing changes due to the amalgamation of churches in our city. This was a tricky direction to go, totally alien to our original philosophy. But at the time, I saw good reason for doing so. Most of the leadership, however, opposed the move. They maintained loyalty to the student ministry as a witness among students. And given the political climate of the time, the idea might not be practical anyway. So there was an impasse. And then the group reached the lowest point in its spiritual life. We somehow decided to devote our energy to studying what the New Testament church was like, especially the way it organized itself. It was hopeless. No one was really interested. At the time, we didn't need that. What's more, it soon dawned on me that the New Testament churches were not that good anyway. But somehow we went on. There was no life. Those who stayed,

stayed out of a sense of obligation. We were hopelessly out of tune. Before we realized it, we were only four.

There was no reason to focus on church polity any more. Not that we had any good reason in the first place. So my wife and I and Sy, a woman instructor in English in her forties, and Yau, a mechanical engineering major about twenty years old, went back to earnest intercession and sharing. We followed our scriptural union daily reading guideline. But I soon gave that up as I got deep into Jeremiah. The others did likewise. We were studying the Bible on our own and we shared our thoughts together. Life on the campus was becoming increasingly frantic. Every student, every family, was engaged in growing vegetables on whatever plot we could find, and soon the call for making steel in one's backyard was raised. But we had peace in our hearts.

One day I came across Pastor Tsai. He had been assigned, for reasons beyond him, to the campus. But he didn't know what he was supposed to do. Nobody was there to supervise him. So he kept himself busy walking around the campus with a small hoe and a watering pot to tend to other people's vegetable plots. People loved him. Anyway, I ran into him and he introduced himself as Pastor Tsai. (It was only during the Cultural Revolution that pastors were called "old uncles".) So I invited him home. As we prayed, he asked if he could celebrate communion together with us. He was Anglican. He asked for wine. We had none. We never dreamed of having wine. We offered tea and he accepted. We had our communion. There was no doctrinal talk. But we had our communion. We felt the real presence of God in our midst. Soon Pastor Tsai became one of us. We never raised the question of the seven doctrinal positions. We never felt the need. Our group had unknowingly turned itself into a church. By 1964, our church had about thirty people worshipping on Wednesdays. Only seven were students or members of the faculty. The others came from the neighbourhood. We had a weekly communion service. Pastor Tsai baptized eight converts, all young people. But they are all gone now.

In the early days of the Cultural Revolution, we suspended our regular worship. Pastor Tsai had been interrogated. Our meeting was known to the Red Guards base. We were afraid. So we decided to pray in our own place.

Later, when I was kicked out of the university, there was no place any more. Like the Jeremiah exiles, we had no temple to go to. We had to worship God in our hearts and in honesty.

The years of the Cultural Revolution were a blank as far as our home meeting was concerned. We had no meeting. I was assigned to work in a fruit-preserving factory, and I lived there. My wife went to live with her parents. There was not much to do. So I was able to visit our church members in their homes. Pastor Tsai was sent to a farm some eighteen kilometres out of the city. In a sense, we could say we had our meetings during visits to my Christian friends. As I was usually free in the mornings, the homes I visited were mostly empty. So we could pray in private, exchange news and encourage one another.

Now I am back teaching physics, and I have also got back my quarters. We have resumed our house worship, but of the twenty we had before the time of the Red Guards, only eight are still around. Five younger people will probably come back eventually from the north-west. However, more new people have joined us. Last Sunday we had over sixty, the largest ever.

Pastor Tsai is working with other pastors to reopen a big church in the city. He's terribly busy, especially in view of his seventy years plus. But he has come back to us on several occasions. Through him we were able to obtain ninety old Bibles and hymnals from the university authorities. So we have some to spare. Can you imagine what that means?

We are over forty kilometres from the city. I guess our group will continue to meet. I am in two minds about our future. On the one hand, I would love to have a pastor come to us, have a small church near the university, and do good evangelism work. On the other hand, I can't help feeling that, given our peculiar situations, it might be best for us to continue to meet in homes, away from the limelight, quietly refracting the light of the Lord. We need to do more intellectual work about our faith. At the moment, we are content. I have my job back, a good salary, respect. But the question still troubles me. What must I do with the propagation of Marxist-Leninism in China? It's not that they are raising the question, simply that I would like very much to know what I should do.

6. "YOUR GOD IS A GOOD GOD"

This is a mining town, and we are some of the finest miners in the country. We hope our church is a good church. We belong to it, love it, and want to share the gospel with others. Everyone in town knows we are Christians and that on Sundays we gather for worship in the morning at ten, and seven-thirty in the evening for those who have to go down the pits. Out of 4000 miners and families, 346, at the last count, were members of this church. We are small in number, but you would never guess that if you come into this place on Sunday. You would think the whole town is Christian, people carrying Bibles and nodding to each other and smiling.

We have been meeting in the Pang Family Clan Hall for years. The Pang clan has been Christian for three or four generations. For a four-year period during the Cultural Revolution, we moved our meetings to one of the miners' dormitories where we could squeeze in about a hundred people. The dormitories were off limits to the Red Guards at first. As they took over the Revolutionary Committee, they could come in, but they never did, and we tried not to get into trouble with them, by not singing too loudly and by including a period of study of the Thoughts of Chairman Mao. Some brothers felt very unhappy about it. But as the Red Guards did not touch us we felt it worthwhile. Once again it was Brother Tang, our leading brother, who helped us see the importance of Christians really living in the world though not of it, the importance of being salt of the earth and light of the world, and not becoming escapists.

Brother Tang is an extraordinary person. He is big and vigorous, in his sixties, and he never seems to tire. He began as a young man working in the pits, gradually moving up to the rank of supervisor. He has education, including college for a year studying theology. Then he told us he had to quit because his father was forced by something or somebody to leave the city. So he settled in and became a miner. This was immediately before the Liberation. In the mine, he got a Bible study group going. The times were chaotic. Brother Tang soon got into trouble with the management and was put in jail a number of times. But the union always got him out. It had to, because he was one of their leaders. Then there was a series of bomb incidents. Tang disappeared. Rumour had it that he had joined the Red Army. But when he reappeared after the Liberation, he did not come back a commissar. He returned to the pit, but his health had deteriorated: a lung problem. So they gave him a desk job to look after the payroll. He retired when he reached fifty-five, and lived on his pension. He came back to the office so often, however, that soon they had him back at work. Meanwhile the Bible study groups continued to expand. They had started coming together on Sundays, about 1958, and gradually became what we are today. Now, our main event is the Sunday worship. The small Bible study groups have dwindled in number. I miss them. But we cannot have everything. What is sure is we need to stick together.

We are fairly well informed of what is going on elsewhere. I think we could have pastors. But then we have Brother Tang, who's more than a pastor to us. In a different sense, we have been lucky too in that we are, and have always been, the only Christian group in town.

We have our Bibles. I suppose almost every family possesses one. We have no Bibles in common. But we brought our Bibles collectively from Peking in 1958 or 1959. When Brother Tang first started the Bible groups, he provided Bibles as well. But when we came together as a church in 1958, we sent someone to Peking with money and bought some 200 Bibles. Then we sold them to our members. We have always had our Bibles. The most difficult period was 1968. The Red Guards were against religion and against Bibles. At one point, they told us that we could have freedom of belief, but our Bible was a travesty of the Precious Book. They meant Chairman Mao's. At that time, every person had the little red book and we walked around with it, and read it out together at the beginning and end of the work day. They would not allow any other book to be treated that way. They wanted to confiscate our Bibles. We finally struck a bargain with them. We would collect all the Bibles, have them put in a place where no one would touch them, and give the Red Guards an inventory, a statement that they were at the disposal of the Revolution Committee. Of course we had custody. We did exactly that, although several Bibles must have got lost somewhere, because soon our people were circulating pages of the Bible. So our church went without the Bible for two or three years. It was a sad and difficult time. For the first time, we had serious internal quarrels.

In the first place, the church leadership was challenged by a group of young miners led by Brother Tu. They felt we had been playing cat and mouse with the Red Guards, that we were not serious in following the highest instructions and the mass line of Chairman Mao. This was a very serious charge. The only solace was that Brother Tu raised it as an internal problem within the fellowship of the church. Nobody could really answer these charges. The so-called highest instructions and mass lines are attitudes and mindsets, and not action or policy, and therefore subject to all kinds of interpretations. Rather unusually, Brother Tang did not respond. Brother Tu and his people kept up their criticism in earnest. They charged us with complacency, with alienation from the masses, and with having lost any sense of idealism. As one of the ruling elders, I finally asked him what they wanted to change. Silence. Then one of the young miners coldly said; "You must step down." He was shouted down. I felt sad. Nothing like this had happened in our church. We were such a happy family. Or were we?

Then eighteen of our young people decided to join a Red Guard Base Brigade going west to propagate Mao thoughts at a predominantly Muslim village. Their parents could not finance the trip. So the matter came before the church. Other young people were as a matter of course financed by the Red Guards Headquarters, whatever it is, or simply went. A group of ninety had previously gone ahead and three had died in the severe cold. So we were not totally against getting some money for the young people. But to our shock, several families strongly objected to our having anything to do with the Red Guards. They cried, and tore their hair, urging us not to let our young people go. Some of their friends and close relatives had suffered greatly in Peking. They had just got word. We became divided. The young people left with some money given by the church. Nobody wanted to talk about it any more. The Cultural Revolution was to divide our church for the next six years. Even now, the pain is still with us. Some feel shame: others feel a sense of loss.

On one occasion, a young girl from one of our families was found to be pregnant. On questioning, she pointed to a Red Guard leader, a popular boy from Peking. And then it was found that hers was not the only case. There was a second case involving another Red Guard. Earlier there had been another girl, but she had an early abortion, so no one except her parents had known. We could not hide this case. News spread. And then it was discovered that some twelve girls in town had got into similar trouble. Parents had hidden these shameful facts from their neighbours. But now that the news was public, people came forward in great anger. Then tragedy struck. One of the girls committed suicide because of the publicity. The townspeople got into a state of feverish anger. Without any planning, a large group of people gathered outside the Red Guards Quarters, rushed into the house, threw the tables around and beat up more than twenty Red Guards who tried to put up a fight. Fortunately nobody died. But soldiers were called in. At first the Guards' leader, a man in his thirties, put up a front, loudly accusing us of bourgeois morality. We shouted him down and threatened to castrate him. From then on, we had little to do with the Red Guards. They did their coordination work and we lived our lives. Life went on. The Red Guards tried to knock us down. But they didn't use violence. Our town was too strong for them. The party cadres and the soldiers kept things relatively calm.

Our church continued to meet. But somehow we felt different. The world had invaded our church. Our young people seemed lost. Our young women were not strong.

The structure of our church? It's very simple really. There are seven of us called elders. At the start, Brother Tang named the seven. Thereafter, the elders worked things out among themselves. When an elder resigns or dies, the other elders would suggest a name and the church would accept the person. We also hold a church business meeting once every three months. There the elders make their reports, and answer questions. The challenge of Brother Tu came this way. The seven elders now in office, of whom I am one, are all miners. I am the youngest at 46. Brother Goo and I are the two preaching elders, because others thought we could preach. The others handle things they can do best — finance, visits, manpower. There are no fixed assignments.

Then we have a group of leaders whom we entrust with certain responsibilities, mainly to keep in touch with people. We all meet on occasion to talk about the church.

Our worship is equally simple. On an average, we have 150 people at the morning worship, and sixty at the evening. We always begin with a few hymns from the Hymns of Universal Praise. We have a small pedal organ and several accordions. Then it is testimony time. I encourage church members to count their blessings. In most cases, the leaders would have already sounded out the people who want to give testimony. I suspect there is some sort of competition among the leaders as to who can produce the best testimony from among their people. They go around asking: "Has God taught you anything recently?" and people open up.

Ordinarily we have four or five witnesses. Sometimes the people tend to be too long-winded, saying the same things over and over again. The stories vary. Births, deaths, marriages, work injuries, going beyond the work quota, family problems, work problems, etc. A few younger people really read their Bible, and I encourage them to share what they have learned.

After the testimonies, I invite people to praise God or to join in intercession, or to stand up and just say a few helpful words. I emphasize that we must say words in love and our purpose must be to build up and not to show off or make fun of other people. Sometimes one or two respond spontaneously. As a rule, I invite particular persons to lead us in prayer or to say a few words of comfort. Here Brother Tang plays a most important role. He would sometimes, but not always, open his Bible, and on the spot read out the most appropriate verses to go with the testimonies. I am learning from him how to do that. Then it is my turn. I speak for ten minutes, usually on the testimonies, to encourage, strengthen and help the people. But I do not always succeed. Finally, we sing another hymn, and then disperse. We have an offering box by the door. Normally, our weekly offering comes to about RMB$15-20. At present the money goes to paying the rent, restoring the heating system which has worn out, and helping out three families, one of which is a member.

Our happiness depends very much on the situation in the mines. The talking-point today is the new union office in a separate building rather than in the mine administration office. We all like the idea, although the union has now to begin collecting dues again. Five months ago when four miners died in an accident the church became very sad, and Brother Tang gave his testimony in church and cried. We stopped the service and went to the office where many miners had already gathered. Our women boiled tea and made hot buns to feed the men standing in the cold. Next Sunday, two widows and their children came to our church, with some of their friends, to thank us. I invited them to say something, and one widow said: "I am not a believer. I am touched by what you people have done. I and my children will live on bravely." Then Brother Tang sobbed loudly in his seat. His old face became much older. And the woman went to him and said: "Don't cry. Your God is a good God."

7. THE CHURCH AT HOME AND THE CHURCH ON A HILL

We have now a church on a hill, with two services on Sunday, but we also meet in homes. In my case, we meet on a Wednesday — about thirty people. Most of the people who attend it cannot easily get to where the church is, so we meet at a home. Most who come are elderly people. Four are blind and have no relatives, they belong to a home for the blind. It used to be a Christian home; then of course the state took it over. They must have become Christian there, and their faith has stayed with them. I wonder what their sightless eyes have seen in all these years. They arrive and leave together, holding a stick in one hand, the other kept on the shoulder of the one in front. They must have been with us for five years now. In the meeting, apart from trying to catch up with the singing, they never venture a single word. They sit on the edge of the bench, very intense, occasionally nodding their heads, sometimes smiling, absorbing everything as if every word was valuable and every note precious. I have encouraged them to share, but no: "What do I know? I am stupid. I just feel happy listening to you." Then they leave together.

They did ask me if I could help them get to church on Sunday. I promised I would try. First the Home must agree. I don't think they would oppose it there. But it does mean a change, and that could take a lot of time. Then I would have to find people to take them. When we have the choir organized, maybe we could do that. The choir is the equivalent of the youth fellowship in our case.

The rest of us are mostly old women in our sixties and seventies, two over eighty. In the case of some, the children are overseas in North America, Singapore, Malaysia. During the past year, we have had visitors almost every other week, visiting their parents and relatives. Their presence gives us great joy. And to see the happy expressions on the faces of these old women is enough to make us shout alleluia. But these visits also pose problems for us. A month ago, after the meeting, one of the blind people asked me to take her to talk to the visitor from America. I did. She began right away to cling to the visitor, a Chinese woman, engaged in a long-winded monologue. I suppose she was asking for something. Everyone was embarrassed.

There are also two teenagers in our group. Very attentive and gentle, carrying their own New Testament. They are fairly new to us. On one occasion I casually remarked that they should go to the church on Sunday rather than come here on Wednesday, because they could find a lot more young people there. They didn't seem to like it. For the next two Wednesdays, they did not show up. I thought they had gone to the church on the hill. But they hadn't. When they came again, they gently confided in me that their grandfather did not want them to go to the public service. Then it was all clear to me. I know their grandfather — an elderly, very cultured person. He used to teach English at the university here. He had suffered much. He had been very much humiliated by the Red Guards. We all were, but maybe not as much as he, a teacher of English and a Christian. I could understand his feelings. When Pastor Yau visited him to discuss with him the reopening of the church, he did not respond. We agreed that the best way was to let him be, looking towards the day when he would join us in worshipping God. So I did not refer to the church any more to his grandchildren. I hope these two young people will find out what is best for them.

Before the church was reopened, our group had another three families. But they have decided to go to the church. So all is well. We call ourselves a meeting point. But in a sense, it is a real church too — wherever two or three are gathered in his name. I am a layman. I have a family of three children. My father was a pastor in this area. He died in 1979. So I assumed the leadership of this group in my home. I do not know what will become of this group. My whole family goes to church on Sundays, and I lead this Wednesday meeting. The old people need this. And who are we to deprive them of a chance to worship God? Or to deprive the two teenagers? There are quite a number of such groups in this city. The church is full to the brim. So we all serve in our different ways. Naturally, there are tensions, I do not deny that. There is no end to suspicion until we begin to pray together. For the life of me, I just cannot see how a genuine Christian can refuse fellowship with others. Anyone can feel the presence of the Spirit as we pray and sing on Sundays in our church on the hill.

There is no such problem with my group. I have a tape-recorder. So I tape the choir presentation from the church service and play it back on Wednesday. Sometimes I tape the sermons too. But I do not always play them back; since they are a bit too long for my group and the recording is not good enough.

Not too long ago, something memorable happened to us. Tang Four Sister, one of us, received a Bible through the mail from her sister in Hong Kong. She could not read it because she is ninety per cent illiterate. But she brought it with her to church anyway. And she had sewed a beautiful cloth bag to carry it in. Everyone admired the bag. We called it a Bible bag, and soon everyone wanted one. It is quite a sight on Sundays to see the old and the young going up the hill towards the church, each carrying a Bible bag. Tang Four Sister is still making her Bible bags. People come to her with a piece of cloth and ask her to make one for them.

The Bible is indeed most dear to us. As I said, when my father died, I took over the group. There were only two other people left. But we prayed. A few years later, we grew to this present number. And all this time, I was simply reading my New Testament to the group, slowly and clearly, and then we prayed for each other and that's about all we did. Now that the situation has changed, I learn to preach a little. I never gave up my Bible. In our area, during the Red Guards era, the church and church workers' homes were thoroughly searched. Their Bibles were taken away. I am a layman. They did not ask me that many questions. I turned over our family Bible. But I kept the New Testament.

My estimate is that every Christian family has a Bible now. Public Security returned some 150 old Bibles to us when we got back our church. I think we have reached a point where we can get by with what we have. And the situation is improving. Shanghai, I understand, will soon be printing Bibles. And we will be able to buy some more. If one knows the trick, one can fairly easily buy new Bibles on the black market for about RMB$10-15. These Bibles must have been smuggled in and the people must be making a lot of money. This is very sad. We have religious freedom. But most of the people are not religious. Some are atheists. Christians and the Christian faith are still very vulnerable to criticism by the masses.

About a year ago, a young girl of eighteen became Christian all of sudden. She was so enthusiastic, she loudly proclaimed the faith. Her parents were opposed to her conversion. As she began telling her neighbours about Jesus Christ, her parents became even more agitated: probably they feared loss of face. They went to the pastor and said many foul words. Finally, they went to Public Security, and demanded investigation into "religious subversion". They behaved most unreasonably. But the police came and spent many days investigating how the young girl became what she was. We protested. The police cadre said they were not interested but had to do it. Fortunately the rest of the townspeople did not take the matter seriously. Some openly mocked the couple, saying that their real motive was fear of not having anyone kowtow to them at their gravestone. Soon the matter subsided. But the whole matter really caught us by surprise. We who are bearers of the name of Jesus must learn to be doubly careful and sensitive.

Concerning the Catholics in this town, I do not know much about them. They also have a church now. Two old ladies in our Wednesday meeting are Catholics. They live on the same street so Sister Tse brings them along. We never thought of them as different. They fit in well with us. I suspect there are more Catholic people than Protestant people in town. I don't know for sure. I know their situation is complex.

I know Catholics and Christians are coming much closer now in churches all over the world. This has not yet happened in this country. Maybe it will, given time. But I doubt it. However, these many years must have made us all more open to God and more eager to learn wherein lies the strength of the other. How could anybody have guessed that I would be preaching today, and serving as "amateur" pastor, reading the scriptures and praying for the coming of the kingdom of God.

8. LOVING GOD AND LOVING PEOPLE

We are eight Christian families and five young people. We have all been peasants for generations. I am the head of the church. Many years ago, we had a pastor who used to come to us every other Sunday. He had five rural churches under his care. Then one Sunday in 1958, he did not show up. We waited and waited, but he did not come. So we dispersed. We contacted the other churches, but he had not been there either. We were very worried for the whole week. The next Sunday, the pastor showed up just as we were about to start our worship. We told him how worried we were. He asked us to proceed as usual, without him. You see, on that particular Sunday, he was not supposed to be with us. We insisted that he take the service. But he would not. So we went ahead — singing, praying and repenting. At one time, the pastor was quietly sobbing. So I knew something was wrong. At the end of the service, he stepped forward, lay his hands on our heads, mine and my wife's, and consecrated us shepherds of the sheep. We were surprised. But we did not protest, seeing the determination on his face. From that point on, I have taken care of this church, not always very well. But God has protected us and guided us.

After the service, the pastor came home with us to teach us how to conduct the Lord's table and say the blessings. "How about preaching?" my wife asked. We all laughed. After so many years, we already knew the words of the Lord's table by heart. But somehow my wife and I never quite got it right that day. We were simply too nervous. Finally, the pastor gave up. "You know it anyway. Do not worry about what to say or how to say it. The Holy Spirit will put words into your mouth." I remember it was getting dark. So we insisted that he stay for supper. After much persuasion, he accepted, but only on the condition that we would not kill a chicken for him. So my wife killed a cockerel for the meal.

After the pastor had gone, our church got into trouble almost right away. A family group next to the church claimed the property, saying it was their land and that missionaries long ago had bought it illegally. As Pastor Tam wasn't around, and since I could not produce the deeds, we had a serious problem. Neither of us could produce any documents. So we stood facing each other.

The deadlock was resolved when we were approached by the branch party secretary for the use of the church as a school for the commune kids. We thought it was not a bad idea as we could still use it on Sundays. Soon, however, we could not do that any more. You just could not pray and sing praises to God while another group was next to you studying newspaper editorials. Besides it did not look nice not to take part in those discussions. So Sunday 4 p.m. was out. The church moved into our house and we met at seven in the evening. It was not a good time, but it was the best we could find.

Most of the year, we begin working in the fields before sunrise. We work in the fields until about one or two in the afternoon, with a meal at eleven under the tree. Then we go home and work at the vegetables and fowls for an hour or so.

In those days, however, twice a week, we had political lessons at 4 p.m., going on until about 6. By that time, we were so tired we could hardly walk. So meeting at seven in the evening was not good. But what else could we have done? Some families stopped coming. I don't blame them. Then Brother Wan and his wife started a prayer meeting very early in the morning around five o'clock. They might have felt I was not a proper pastor. They were right of course. But we kept our friendship. In these several ways, our church became smaller in number. By the time of the terrible flood in 1964, we had only about twenty people in our midst.

We have always had floods. Immediately after the Liberation, three flood control dams were built successively and we enjoyed good harvests. But then things turned bad. First the woodlands around the dams disappeared. People simply chopped down the trees. At the time, much wood was needed to fuel the back-garden furnaces for steel. And then the sandbags on the upper levels of the dams were systematically taken away for other projects. We protested, but to no avail. Then in 1964, we had two weeks of continuous rain. When the water burst through, it could not be stopped. It wiped out everything in its path — the crops, houses, barns, roads. Over two hundred died in the village. Our cottage was saved, but the crops and even the topsoil were gone. The topsoil was deposited in a shallow valley some five kilometres away. The years that followed were the toughest years for our church and for our commune. We are in a much better situation now. But when we look back at those years, many of us cannot help crying.

First we had to bury the dead. One would never have imagined how much the dead weighed and how foul they smelled. Nobody wanted the job. We were all emaciated by then, sick in body and in heart. Most refused to touch the bodies for religious reasons. That left only a handful of cadres and the Christians, and the relatives. So we began digging. There was no time to lose if we were to continue to live in the village and not be killed by diseases. Surrounded by the sight and smell of those bloated bodies, my first prayer was for the Lord to return immediately, to lift up these dead and to restore human shape to the decaying flesh. The relatives dug the graves too. It must have been doubly difficult for them. Soon everybody simply dug and dumped the bodies into the graves. On many occasions, I called the Christians together for prayer. We needed to find out how my people were doing. And we all needed each other. At the prayers, I did not know what to say except that Jesus cried over the dead and that he must be with us on the spot. There were others too who had joined us. I did not hear them pray. But they were there, their eyes spoke, shouted. I felt I needed to know what to say to these people, but I didn't know.

Food was scarce. Five truckloads of flour, beans and medicine arrived. We had a little respite. But the trucks never returned. Soon we were reduced to eating a mixture of flour, sweet potato stalk and tiny fish and crab ground into a paste. Hunting for food was the only activity left for people in the village. Some in the family went out to find food, others remained in the house to guard whatever they still possessed. Not that there was much, nor that there was fear of violence. But petty thievery was common. What else do you do when you see your children contract in pain for lack of food and then quietly groan all night long? There were, to be sure, occasional excitements. As when someone's son had his leg broken when he went to a neighbouring village, probably while trying to steal food. Or a common meal when relief came in from the city, but in too small a quantity to be distributed.

Of course Christians also went about on empty stomachs. The flooding took two of us back to the heavenly home. When we recognized their bodies in the mud, we saw two peaceful faces. They were father and son. They left behind a widow and four children. Our Christian women stayed with the family for several weeks afterwards.

Our worship meetings continued. But we were down to twelve. Most of the time, our prayers were prayers of repentance. We examined ourselves according to the Ten Commandments, really opening up our hearts to see where we had sinned. We had nowhere to turn except to God. Soon many more people began coming to our church. They did not know much about Jesus. We told them about Jesus in hymns and Bible stories and they nodded their heads. But then, after the service, they would go to a Taoist den and do the same thing. Whatever the reason, many showed up at the Sunday service, sometimes up to a hundred. Probably half of them genuine believers.

In 1966, my wife passed away. She had been eating very little, letting me and the boys eat. She had become very weak. Then she just could not hold on, and Jesus called her home. She died of starvation. We held a service to remember her. I did not officiate until towards the end when the Lord's table was set. As I reached into the jar for the dry, thin biscuits, I realized there weren't enough to go round. My wife who made these biscuits had always seen to it that there was enough for everyone. But now she was gone. So I had to ask every four persons to share one biscuit. It was embarrassing. I still cannot figure out how she had managed to provide enough biscuits for the Lord's table when food was so scarce — unless she had added her own share.

Things gradually improved. By 1968, the village returned to a more or less normal state. But we are still very poor. The Cultural Revolution did not get to us. Apart from some of our young people not going into the field, pretending to be doing revolution and making fools of themselves, we were never seriously affected. Our meetings continued at my place, at the back of the house where we would not be disturbed. Every Sunday, we have about 100 to 150 people, depending on the season and the work load.

The Bibles, they were never taken away from us. Most of the Bibles we have now are worn out. The flood spoiled everything including the Bibles. I think we lost over forty. Our people rescued the rest and made new cloth covers for them from sandbags.

Preaching has always been difficult for me. I can read and write. And I remember old sermons well. But I don't know how to preach well. So I concentrate on several scriptural parts. The Ten Commandments are extremely important for us. I preach about them many many times. And I always manage to find something new to say. I must have preached twenty times on each of the Ten Commandments. And we also repent according to the Ten Commandments. I can also preach on the Eight Blessings and the curses, the Lord's Prayer, and the parables. That's about it, along with gospel stories and some psalms of course. That's about what I have been preaching on these many years. Sometimes I wanted to preach on Paul. But then I would find that I had nothing more to say than reading his letters out loud. There are a number of committed young peasants in my church. Their intercessions are quite well worded. Sometimes I thought I should let them preach. They could speak better than I could in public. But I hesitated, and decided against it. They do not know the Bible that well. And there are so many pagan religious people around that one can never be sure what is in young people's minds nowadays. What we hope of the Three-Self Patriotic Movement is that they come and teach us or train our young.

I have a terrible story about a young soothsayer by the name of Choi. He is a very smart fellow, no more than thirty. He had lost both his parents in the war and made a living by selling medicinal herbs. He soon began peddling animal bone powder and his own cocoction of miracle waters and pastes. He claims certain medicines are good for certain people born during certain months and under certain celestial influences. He would go around the village and, suddenly getting hold of a person, would warn him of deadly diseases deep within his abdomen and so on.

One day Choi showed up at the church service and listened attentively. He came three more times and then he asked to be baptized. He said he believed in the Christian God. I became suspicious and asked him if he believed in Jesus. He said he did wholeheartedly. Finally I asked him if he would give up his soothsaying. He wouldn't say yes. He hesitated. Then he said that it was the spirits which told him to come to the Christian church. He could not give them up. So I said no, with regret to his request. We could not accept him into the church. Several younger people in the church asked me to reconsider the decision. They were unhappy about my refusal to baptize him. It turned out Choi had been playing medium with them, drawing them into contact with the spirits in hell. On learning of this, I was even more determined not to baptize him. The young people were not happy. But they could do nothing. So Choi was out. Then he turned vengeful. He openly declared war on Christianity. He began to say to the villagers that he was more powerful than Jesus Christ. He made nasty jokes about our Lord. When we gathered for fellowship and worship, he would curse us loudly and publicly outside the church. Somehow he got hold of a Bible and openly pissed on it. I was so angry that I and a few other Christians rushed out and threatened to beat him up. He fled and did not come again. But word soon spread that he had put a spell on every member of my church, and a special deadly spell on me in particular. Some villagers reportedly saw him perform curse rituals in his own house. He had warned them not to poke their heads into his room as it had become the temporary abode of evil spirits.

We disregarded him of course. But soon we noticed our neighbours beginning to keep a distance from us. They had heard him warn of the intrusion of evil spirits into our bodies. This had an effect on some of us. Two elderly women from our church had fever. They said meaningless things about the spirits in their sleep. When one of our babies developed a big sore on the head, people whispered about the spirits. It was becoming to be impossible. I had nobody to consult. The pastor was not here. My wife had died. I didn't know what to do. Even some old-timers were wavering. The soothsayer did not come out of his house now. All the doors and windows were closed. He had locked himself in, according to his neighbours, in order to bring the last curses on us.

His final act before he went into seclusion was to place an evil spell on his rooftop, towards the direction of the church. I led a protest group to the commune secretary. He would not listen. It was just one superstition against another.

It was useless. We all went home. I was deeply grieved. I fell on my knees for guidance. No guidance came. Later, as I began to prepare my sermon, my mind suddenly came up with the First Commandment. You shall have no other gods before me. Suddenly, light came through. We worship Jehovah as God, the only God. The other gods are not really gods. Then I fell on my knees again, and it became plain, as I said it out loud: "God, we promised to worship you alone, and have done so. You must protect us from other gods." It was so clear. The cloud had lifted. I called the Christian people together right away. I reminded them of the First Commandment. We were about sixty, as quite a few were still in the fields. People understood. Our God is the only God. We were relieved, free. Then I led the whole group to Choi's house. The door and windows were shut. I kept the First Commandment in my heart as I and a few others pushed open the door. Choi was in there, frightened, beside a cursed candle. He had a sacrifice bowl. The torn Bible was beside it. I suppose he had been burning Bible pages. He shouted madly at us not to touch him and his things, warning us of the spirits. We were not scared. Armed with the First Commandment in our hearts, we took the Bible, ground to pieces the bowl and the charms and destroyed the candle. Choi was too frightened to put up a fight. I warned him that Jehovah our God is the only God, and that he must not call evil spirits upon us again. He said he would go to the leading cadre. We laughed and left in triumph and in freedom. A big load fell off my heart. Our

God is God. As we came out, we were almost cheering, every single person, men and women, old and young. But there was a much greater surprise: almost the whole village was there watching us. As we cheered, they also cheered and clapped their hands. One shouted: "You forget the curse on the rooftop?" I laughed and got a young man to climb up there and take it down. Another loud cheer from everyone. We had proclaimed the First Commandment.

Choi is not a problem any more. The leading cadre made a stern announcement that no person would be allowed to cast a spell on anyone. We agreed. This led to our being given some interesting duties. There were many religious rites in the village and old women made a little money selling joss sticks, paper charms and so on. Now somebody had to investigate as to which would be carriers of curses. The job fell to several of the Christians. One of them is a teacher. He found this work very amusing, and he has been entertaining us with funny stories about this business since then. His report was good. He wrote at one point: "Christianity does not put curses on other people." I told the teacher it wasn't quite true. Jesus did curse two-faced people. But of course we understood each other.

This is important for Christianity. Superstition is bad. And superstition involving evil spirits is even worse. But Christianity is no superstition. Christianity helps us not to be dependent on superstitions. I have seen what superstition does to people. People losing their minds. Hurting their own bodies and their children. Frightening their neighbours. Throwing good money away. The Communist Party is right to oppose superstition. But now superstition seems to be coming back. I am worried. I hope our church can show the light of Jesus in the darkness of superstition.

We are better off now. You look at us from the high ground across the river, and you see patches of green near every house. We have vegetables, poultry and pigs. Now our stomachs are full. We have two hot meals every day. Every house has a bicycle, two in some cases. This is very important. People can stay on in church and talk to each other. We now can eat together and celebrate without the fear that some families do not have any food to contribute. The old people are singing more loudly. But when we eat, we remember the old days and cannot forget God who even then provided for us. We pray for spiritual food, and for a good pastor to come to us. Soon our young people will be bored with my Ten Commandment sermons.

No, you don't want to hear my First Commandment sermons. I am not a cultured man. The first Commandment is God speaking to the Jews who had nowhere to go. The Jews were desperate. God wanted them to live, and he would help them. So he lay down ten conditions for them. The first is that they must not worship idols. Idols depend on people for food. But people depend on God. Now we have food, this shows God has kept his promise to us because we worship him. The communists do not believe in God. They do not believe in idols either. So they are not slaves of evil gods. And they obey some commandments. The important thing is we listen to Jehovah God. If we listen, we will hear God speaking to us, and we will then obey him. But if we don't listen to God, or only hear of him from some other people, then we do not hear God speaking to us. "You shall have no other gods before me." God is speaking to you. Have you ever heard God speaking to you? This is the key. I have heard God speak to me. Once you have heard God speak, you don't forget. Many people do not hear God speak. You see, nobody can see God. If you see God, you die. So the only possible thing is to hear God. Some people do not hear God because they have other gods between them and God. It could also be that God speaks in a very quiet voice. You cannot hear him if there are other gods already speaking in your ear. Well, these are my First Commandment sermons. But I often mention this even when I am preaching on other commandments.

The Sermon on the Mount is Jesus' Ten Commandments. The Lord's Prayer is our Ten Commandments to God given to us by Jesus. And so on. The chief thing, I believe, is that we deeply love God and love our people. For generations, my family has tried to love God and love the people in this village. It's very different now. The new water ways and dams have altered the landscape quite a bit. But our faith and our church have not altered. Even if the pastor should come back, he would still be able to recognize our services and our songs.

9. A CHRISTIAN VILLAGE

I am eighteen years old. My parents, foster parents actually, have asked me to tell you about our church and our community. Not because they don't want to do it themselves but because they feel my Mandarin is better than theirs. Also I have been with the church since I was two years old and I know it quite well. We are a small Korean minority community of about eighty families. There is a much larger one some fifty kilometres away with over 400 families. In our case, we are all Christian. The heads of the households make a solemn pledge every year at Easter that our whole village will live for ever in devotion to our Lord Jesus Christ. Then it is the young people's turn. Last year, the weather was freezing. Nevertheless, we had our traditional Easter outdoor sevice early in the morning. It was still dark; I could not count the number of people there. We could not sing at all; it was too cold. We raised high our arms and prayed, received special blessings from the elders, and returned to our homes.

Pastor John Tsai has been our pastor for many years. He's been with us right from the beginning. For the past three years, however, he has not been able to leave his house, so he blesses the buns and the wine, and the deacons carry them into the church, and we have the fellowship of the holy communion. We have fixed a loudspeaker in his room so he can follow the service. We have a big room across the open courtyard, capable of seating sixty people along the four walls. Other people bring small wooden stools, so we can seat about 120 altogether in three rows all around. We have been thinking of putting in benches, but wood is difficult to come by.

Pastor Tsai is not Korean, he is a Han. I was told that he used to work with the big church in Shenyang. But when the Korean church fell into difficulties with the authorities in 1952, Pastor Tsai helped work things out, and so, when one day our Korean friends introduced him to us, we welcomed him. He's been pastor at our church since then. Pastor Tsai's wife died in the late sixties. I was only six, but I took part in the mourning and comforting week; I was in charge of providing hot tea to those who came in to sit with Pastor Tsai. If it had not been for Pastor Tsai's insistence, it would have gone on beyond the one week. Pastor Tsai is that much respected in the community. Of his three sons, two are working elsewhere and have their families, but they come back at the New Year; the middle one died in the Korean war.

About eight years ago, Lee Big Sister came to us from Korea where she had been ministering to Christian groups. As we grew in number and saw Pastor Tsai's health beginning to fail, we contacted our friends and relatives in Korea and were able to get her to come over and serve us.

Our village community, I am told, began in the early years of the century when many Koreans were brought in by the Japanese to work in the new steel mills and, farther north, in the timber industries. Some were lucky to have their families with them, some joined them later. Some married local girls. But from the start, even up to the Liberation, relationships between us and the Han people were not good. You see, we were brought in to work in the mills because the Japanese did not trust the Hans at the time. And, of course, Koreans did not like the Hans either. They would not let us move into the town. And so we had our settlement here. But now the town has extended itself, and so we are very much part of it. After the Liberation, we received much better treatment. The cadres were kind to us: after all we belong to China and many were born here. We were also given train tickets to pay short visits to our relatives and when we got into the train, we found gift parcels of food and fruits on the seats.

The American war in Korea was bad. Our motherland was almost swallowed up by the Americans until Chairman Mao permitted volunteers to move across the river border. To be sure, the Party gave us support. A lot of Chinese volunteered, and of course our community did. My father said some fifty young Korean men went to fight. Ten did not return, not even their bone ashes. The families received medals and a sum of money. Today some of us still hate American imperialists.

My real father's family name is Tsou. He was a welder. When I was two, he was killed in an accident. My mother, whom I can hardly remember now, wanted very much to go home to her relatives in Korea. But then she probably had to make a child bride of me, otherwise who would want to spend money to feed another family's girl? She did not want to do this. Then my foster parents came along and offered to bring me up, provided I took their name. They had no child of their own. And their wanting me to carry their name guaranteed that I would not be made a child bride. So my mother agreed and went home. She did not write back. A few years later word came through that she had married, and wanted me to be obedient to my foster parents.

My foster parents are very kind people. Both are deeply pious Christians. As an elder, my father is one of the leaders of the church and of the community. One of his tasks is to see to it that parents bring up their children in the Christian way. He is so conscientious that at one time he had a class at home for young parents on Christian parenthood. He still takes special pains to call in the young people one by one to have long talks with them. His other regular task is the morning prayer at 6:30 every day for some twenty families in the neighbourhood. Normally four or five show up, sometimes ten. I did not attend until I was fifteen. After I was fifteen, I grew up much quicker. I became aware of the problems of the church and of my neighbours. My father is a very different person when he is praying. Normally he is very strict, and capable. People come to him for all kinds of advice. But when praying, he is much gentler, and he does not scold people.

One of our present problems is who our next pastor should be. The people do not agree. Some want a man. Some feel that after so many years of faithful service, Lee Big Sister ought to be made pastor. These people point out that women pastors are not uncommon. My father has not said much on the subject. My feeling is he is probably in favour of having a man. Pastor Tsai stayed away from the discussion. He would like to see us consult other Christian people in the province.

Three years ago, our church had a terrible time. Elder Chong, one of the oldest of the elders, was accused by his unit (in the steel plant) of conspiracy to default. Apparently, as a top engineering worker, he had managerial responsibilities. As they were going through the books they found a lot of irregularities. Elder Chong wanted to speak to the church after a Sunday service. So we ate our hot noodles as we listened to him. He said that he had not cheated. He had no extra money. (My father confirmed that.) But very probably there were irregularities for which he could be held responsible. His wife angrily jumped up and defended him. She said that during the Cultural Revolution, it would be irregular not to have irregularities. It was a time of power play and her husband was a victim. It was a very emotional meeting. Elder Chong finished, tendered his resignation so as not to tarnish the name of the church and asked us to intercede for him. News of the scandal spread, and vicious rumours about Elder Chong and his associates rose from many quarters. Most of the church people were behind him, but a number wavered. After some months, Elder Chong was demoted by four points at his job, and that was the end of the story. It was completely unjust. Nobody knew what actually happened; certainly not a young girl like me. I respect him as an elder. He is always an elder to me.

My father told me specifically to tell our evangelism story. Eight or nine years ago, our village was not all Christian. My blood mother was not a Christian. We had a lot of problems among us. Some wives are of Korean blood, some Han. One of the problems, I understand, had to do with coke. We depend on coke for fuel to keep our room warm. It so happened that the Korean women felt that the Han women were getting better quality coke, in bigger pieces and at the same price, thanks to their family ties with those in charge. This was the beginning. Soon the men were drawn in. It was bad. People did not talk to each other.

The crisis came during an extremely cold winter. A baby boy died in the night. The mother almost went crazy. She made wild accusations regarding the quality of the coke and why it went dead in the middle of the night. Things became very tense. The heads of the families came together to deal with the accusation and find a solution to the matter of coke distribution. There were Christians on both sides. For some time, the discussion got nowhere. Then Brother Lee, whose wife is Han, volunteered to share his coke with others. Nobody took him seriously. But he did what he promised. After work hours, he would bring a few kilos of coke and give it to a Korean family. Nobody knew what game he was playing. He simply walked in, gave his greetings and said: "I've come to see if you need coke. This is fine coke." If there was no response, he would simply leave the coke by the stove and go away. Sometimes they would examine the coke, chat about its quality and have tea. One Sunday, after the service, Elder Chong asked Brother Lee to come up. He embraced him in front of everybody, and told the church what Brother Lee had done. He said: "Brother Lee alone acted like our Lord. He showed us the way." Brother Lee was moved to tears. Elder Chong could not contain himself either. Soon everybody was crying and confessing their sins to each other.

Some time later, the heads of the families came together to continue their negotiations. My father said that about two-thirds were not Christians then. At the meeting, the Christians from both sides offered to share their coke, not just once but always. It broke the stalemate. Within a year, according to my father, all the family heads became Christian and were baptized. And they took their wives and children into the church as well. This was how ours became a Christian village.

Evangelism is very important for us. Father insists that it must begin with the heads of families; otherwise, he reasons, what right does he have to be the family head? So he puts in a lot of effort as an elder to get parents to be good Christians and to teach their wives and children about God. When it's his turn to preach, he likes to ask the people to commit themselves to preaching the gospel to their neighbours. He would ask people to raise their hands. He would have a young man take down their names. Later in the week, or the next Sunday, he would get hold of these people one by one and ask them how they were faring.

10. THREE BIBLES AND FIVE SETS OF HYMN SHEETS

I used to be a Lutheran pastor. I am still a pastor, in a church of nine people, including myself and my wife. It's a young church. We began only some eighteen months ago, meeting in my home. There are the Shen couple, in their sixties, more or less our age. There are three strong young men. One understands himself to be a Christian, the others are eager to learn. There is a boy who is literally addicted to the Bible. He's only twelve. A very outspoken Christian. I fear he's going to cause problems for us. But I can't turn him away. No church should turn people away. Then there is big Auntie Kuo. She's in her mid-fifties, a mild mental case. She has no relatives. She never speaks clearly, is partially blind. She prays in a muttering manner. We are not much, but we've grown from three when we first started. Now we have increased three hundred fold!

We have a prayer meeting at 6 every morning. During planting and harvest time, the young men couldn't come. But the others are always present. I begin with a scriptural reading, then we meditate on the words, then we pray for ourselves, for our neighbours or simply praise God. The young people have acquired an interesting habit of imitating the rhythm of the scripture we read. Big Auntie Kuo prays in her own manner, muttering and murmuring without regard for us, moving her filthy head. Once when we found it too much, we boiled a big kettle of water and washed her hair. At first, she resisted. Then I made a sermon out of the experience — on Samson, and Mary Magdelene washing Jesus' feet with her hair. She seemed to understand. Now, it has more or less become a regular ritual. Big Auntie Kuo sometimes brings her own wood for the water. Now, we are also praying for our country, the Party, the four modernizations programme. At first, they didn't know how to pray about these things. China is not people. China does not believe in God. How can we pray? I told them that when they pray for China, they should regard themselves as China, and pray to God accordingly. Imagine! although we are only a few, we represent China in the eyes of God. So we pray, every day at the break of dawn.

On Sunday at 4 in the afternoon, we have our worship service. My wife and the Shens prepare the altar, two small candles, a wooden cross on a bright red sheet. When we first began, I used to make use of a red scarf hanging down from my neck. But when I learned that the newly re-opened church in the city had done away with these symbols, I decided to follow suit. Our form of service is basically Lutheran, but of course nobody in our group would recognize it as such, nor would we call it that. As a matter of fact, we had two Catholic friends with us for some six months. Now they have found their own meeting group. And just as well. I preach every Sunday to the group except on occasions when I would be invited to preach and serve communion to another Christian group some sixteen kilometres away. When I stand up to preach, I feel my life is not in vain. But I also feel ashamed for having been unfaithful to the church of Jesus Christ. I failed to perform my ministerial duties for fifteen years. May God forgive me.

There is no definite order in my sermon. I am getting old. And my mind rusts because of long years of neglect. I have my Bible now. But to share it with others needs so much understanding and interpretation. Looking back on my life, my sermons must have changed a lot in emphasis. I recall the days immediately before the closing down of our church in the late fifties. Lay people wanted to hear sermons on the second coming and suffering. There was pressure from two sides — that we pastors should help Christian people participate in the construction of socialist China, and that God wanted us to prepare Christians for the end of the world, and for suffering. To the extent that we didn't, we would be labelled non-believing. The vehemence of Christians! Being a little person, I was not in the limelight. But I must say we pastors failed in this crucial period to provide for appropriate spiritual nourishment to our flock. We were too negative about life, about the People's Government. Now I try to preach mostly on forgiveness, on forgetting the past and holding hands for the future, on people loving each other on the foundation of God's love for us. My last week's sermon, "Jesus our Friend", and the previous one, "God our Comforter", were both drawn from John's Gospel, chapters 14 and 15. Actually, the last should have been titled, "The Holy Spirit our Comforter", but, God forgive me, I hesitated to use the term the Spirit because I couldn't explain it well to my people, and it is so easy for them to get the Holy Spirit confused with other spirits. Since the downfall of the Gang of Four, spiritualists, witches, fortune-tellers, what have you, have blossomed on all sides. Most, I believe, are sham, an easy way to make money. But, there is no avoiding it, there is power, attraction. People do show an interest. And when they feel despair, they go to them. Just a few days ago, our little twelve-year-old came to me, with his Bible open, and asked me if I could cast out demons. He added that a "spiritual grandma", in the village, probably a Taoist lay-priestess, could. I was tongue-tied. I told him the ability to cast out demons is a gift, and I don't have it. God has ordained me a pastor, a minister of the word of God. He nodded his head, but I could see he was disappointed. When he turned to go, a great fear rushed over me; that the child would be heading towards the home of the spiritualist. I became so emotional, I ran after him, held him in my arms: "Listen, you must listen. Jesus is God. If we know Jesus, we know God. There is no other way, no more to know about God. You understand?" He smiled; I hope he really understands.

There are three Bibles among us and almost five sets of hymn sheets, taken from the original bound copies, incomplete. The two Bibles we got from my cousin in Singapore. He and his wife came to visit me and left their Bibles with us. The third Bible belongs to the twelve-year-old. He said he found it at his house. But his family was never a Christian home. His Bible was interesting, however; a 1953 version printed in Hong Kong. When he first found it, he instantly knew it to be a religious book, so he took it to me and had me read it to him as it was printed in old traditional characters. Soon he got hold of the style and began reading on his own. Then he found we were praying in the morning. He simply came and became part of us. I was without Bibles and commentaries for some twelve years. It was in 1968 that the Red Guards ordered all "poisonous material" collected and placed in the school basketball court. That day, I parted with my last Bible.

My other Bibles and commentaries I had already disposed of secretly a few weeks earlier. I was afraid that what had happened to Comrade Chiang, a teacher in one of our Production Brigade schools, would happen to me. Undoubtedly, he was an old-school type. His pupils and the Red Guards turned against him, putting him inside a bamboo cage, dragging him around with a "cow" label, leaving him uncovered in the courtyard at night, and finally forcing him to eat pages from his remaining book collection, some deliberately smeared with excrement. Chiang was a skeleton when they finished with him after two weeks. He had nowhere to go, as his home had been taken over. I went to the Red Guard command post to seek permission to have him stay with me. They didn't care. So I took him home and nursed him. He ate, but would not talk much. He didn't want to implicate me. After a week or so, one morning, I found him gone, leaving his quilted jacket. I knew instantly what had happened. He had chosen to kill himself. Some time later, his body was found hanging from a tree. That was in 1968. I remember. I can never forget it. I had never felt so worthless, so sinful and so helpless in all my sixty-three years. I could have told him about Jesus. I could have prayed with him. I am supposed to be a minister of the word of God, yet I said nothing to him. May God forgive me and have mercy on his soul.

Things have improved in the last couple of years. People now speak much more freely. I got in touch with the Shens who used to be in my congregation and we began to pray together. Then Chong, their neighbours' twenty-some-year-old son, became interested. So I gave him instruction — it wasn't that easy without my Bible and books, and I dared not then write things down on paper. He decided to seek baptism. So I baptized him at my home. I was moved to do something I had never done before in my ministry as a pastor. After I had baptized Chong, I asked my wife and the Shen couple to form a circle and embrace the young man. My wife cried in joy, soon we all cried and shed happy tears. Chong, who knows quite a bit about the scriptures now, always jokes that he's been baptized with water and with tears. What about the baptism of fire? I wonder.

We are treated with much respect now. Comrade cadre has been calling me comrade pastor and asked if I would prefer to stop being a fishmonger in the coop market, a job I have held since 1974. I said I wanted to go on. This job isn't too physically demanding. I can, of course, afford to devote more time to being a pastor. The commune has been instructed to pay back the rent in arrears from the parsonage since, I don't know, 1967 or 1964. The money will be at my disposal because I am the natural trustee of the property. But I want to go on as I have been. I am an old man. The hearts of the people are restless. I cannot afford another mistake. I have recently decided, together with the Shens and my wife, not to seek the recovery of the parsonage. Three families are living in there right now. The chapel is in a hopeless state. The roof has long fallen down. All the good bricks were taken away. We will continue to meet in our home.

I do not envision great things. I am an old man, not a person who can do big things, in any circumstances. We need help. I have contact with a former co-worker in the Three-Self Movement office. Maybe we can get some help from them in terms of information, literature, training. Meanwhile, my hope is that God will give us peace, peace in our hearts, in the village, in China, world peace. Peace, so that we can continue to pray at the break of dawn.

11. CHRISTIAN NURTURE IS WHAT WE NEED

The chances are good that, if I try, we could repossess what used to be the Lutheran church down by the school and have our worship in there. It would take some time but it could be done, with some help of course. Only that I am too old, seventy-one now, and I am not sure how the Christians would react. What if we have a big church with a 300-seat capacity, and then Christians quarrel all over? There is religious ferment, no doubt about it. Nearly half of the shops along South Willow Road are selling joss sticks, doing a brisk trade. People are openly reading palms; it is good business in the night market. And nobody in authority bothers to say anything. Actually many far from harmless religious activities are going on in town. The aged Taoist nun has reappeared, taking in young virgins in exorcism rites. Some silly women are only too eager to volunteer their daughters. The money is good, I am told.

I am too old to start a church again. I am simply not up to getting the whole thing organized, dealing with occupants, quarrelsome Christians, and a thousand chores. Several weeks ago, I went into the city to be with my son and his family. I went with them to Hay Ling Church. The pastor and I were old friends. He asked me about our situation and I told him about the problems. He was rather encouraging, and scolded me for not trying.

There are three groups of Protestants meeting in town. There is also a Catholic village nearby, led by a priest who belongs to a family with thirteen grown-up children, very devoted Catholics and influential among the villagers. I am not strictly speaking a member of any one of the three Protestant groups. With two, I am close. But not so much with the third. They let me in on their worship as a worshipper. But the inner circles have their own separate communion table. So full fellowship is out. I recently talked to the head, Deacon Yin, about the possibilities of church premises. He liked the idea and told me they would very much like to have use of some meeting place on Sunday. But there was no way this group would worship with the other two. So let them be.

It is because of situations like this that I hesitate to claim the church premises. During all these years, I would say most Christians in the town, about four or five hundred, have learned to dismiss their denominational biases and are happy to come together if some place is available.

Last Christmas, I got the school hall for carol-singing and celebration. The Sze Kwong group and On Lok group (named after the respective streets on which their meeting places are located) took charge of it together, and presented some very good singing, and candy gifts for every child. Over five hundred showed up, filling the hall. After that the leading cadre had a friendly meeting with us, asking if we could do this cultural thing once or twice a year. The town would cover the cost. We quickly said yes. Now a combined choir is rehearsing regularly. Many young people want to join the choir, and when questioned by us, claim an interest in Christianity. I and Pastor Hsu and Deacon Fung, who lead the two groups, decided that we should be extremely cautious. One must have a firm foundation in the faith and one should be mature enough to explain one's decision to one's parents who might object. Becoming a Christian is not a trivial matter. We should not take it lightly. Anyway, my point is that there is no problem in the Sze Kwong and On Lok groups coming together. Deacon Yin's group is different. They believe that Christmas is a pagan festival and that Christians should repent rather than celebrate on the day. Repentance is fine. We must repent every day. But so should we celebrate every day. Even in the midst of death and suffering. I do not see how after all these many years we can draw in Deacon Yin. Not that he's a bad man. Not at all. He's kind, when he's not preaching.

Let me describe Deacon Yin and his people. There are about forty, all quite old, with a few twenty-year-olds. Of course he's of the Little Flock background, a branch of it. He used to own a fairly big plant turning out soap, fragrant water, etc. The Christian Assembly, as a church, also owned a number of business enterprises elsewhere. They still own a small metal shop with twenty workers making watchbands. So financially they are in good shape. Deacon Yin has suffered much, and suffering has hardened his heart. The other day, as we were talking about the possibilities of getting the church premises back, he suddenly hardened, and without the least provocation on my part, let fly these angry words: "I've washed my bottom clean in preparation for jail if you force us to worship together." The words and tone were so uncharacteristic of the gentle, cultured man he is. He was not accusing me or anyone in particular. He knew that his group has as much right to religious freedom as anyone else. And he is not the kind of person who would let his rights be taken away without a fight. I do not understand his behaviour. He still sees Christians in terms of believing and unbelieving. But he would not make any assessment of individuals. To me it's so pointless and futile. After so many years of testing and testing, how can one fail to see the hand of God in everyone who professes his name? And even in those of us who at one point or another denied Jesus in word and behaviour. Isn't there forgiveness enough to draw them back? Deacon Yin's suffering has hardened his heart.

For most of us, I would say the years have softened and opened us to other people and to God. Pastor Hsu, Methodist-trained, at one time in the fifties was widely accused by Christians in private as non-believing and being a willing consort of anti-Christ atheism. He was young then, but heartbroken. And now, about sixty, the man is our hope. The Sze Kwong group is almost two hundred on Sundays. Not all are Christians, of course. It meets in a semi-covered courtyard by his house. I asked him to take the initiative in claiming back the Lutheran church premises. This will give us room to expand. But he hesitated. The pain that some Christians inflicted upon him in the past is still there with him. I have a wicked thought. Let the old die, and with them past bitterness, mistakes, divisiveness. On the other hand, the past cannot return to us without some profit.

I do not know the On Lok group as well except by contact when I was invited to preach the occasional sermon. It has about sixty people, a very prayerful group. When they pray, they all kneel, not worrying about passers-by. Pastor Fung is a friend, but I find it difficult to feel at home with his adventist style. Brought up a Baptist, I just do not find it easy to talk about signs. Christianity is not going to be a spectacular tree in China, tall, gorgeous, powerful. But something like a seed lying in the soil, growing into a shrub, spreading wide in all directions.

I don't think we can call the three groups home or house churches. There are 260 people in them. Far too big. Before the liberation, my church used to have home meetings, dividing up the congregation into groups of ten, meeting at homes of lay people for mutual care. It was good, except that we inevitably had to meet in well-to-do homes. There was little choice in terms of space, privacy and the provision of snacks. This made the poorer Christians feel uneasy. So it was not the ideal situation.

How I wish we could have small home meetings in which Christians will learn to support each other. But so far I cannot see how this may happen. Space and privacy are both necessary. Some of the homes still have two or three families living in them, and we must respect their feelings. Non-believers pose another problem. You see, we must not hole ourselves up away from the community. Yet a neighbour who has no Christian experience and who would like to take part makes the situation rather difficult. In our case, it is not always easy to say who is a Christian and who is not. There are people in Sze Kwong who have been with us for a year or two, and who participate in everything including communion, but are yet to be baptized. (The On Lok group is more strict regarding communion.) They believe in Jesus, and they say so publicly. But when, for example, a young woman, who worked in one of the consumer co-ops, was asked by her supervisor if she had a religion, she said no, and then quietly added: "I believe in Jesus Christ." You see, in some units, being "Christian" still carries class or social connotations.

But the main reason why I do not see small home meetings coming into being among our churches is the lack of leadership. We simply do not have people who have enough biblical knowledge to do the job. Not that I believe one must be trained in a seminary. After so many years without much Christian teaching, we cannot expect too much. Probably the same is true even of ordained people like us.

Take Deacon Yin's grandson. He's a young man, maybe thirty-five. He's destined to succeed Deacon Yin. You know what he's saying over and over again in his sermons? He says that grace is everything. It is grace that saves and sustains us. And nothing else matters. Faith is totally divorced from conduct. Christ on the cross overshadows us and everything we do. Our thoughts and actions don't matter. If they matter at all, they are totally corrupt and sinful. It is grace that covers us. In fact, man does not matter. Man does not exist. God sees only Jesus Christ, not us. And we should rejoice, because human beings are filthy, rotten to the core. This is the message. I can understand the experience behind it. But it is neither biblical nor edifying. What effect will this have on a young mind? I tremble when I think of it.

I am not that concerned about correcting him. I am unlikely to succeed in any case. I am concerned how we who are pastors could properly feed the sheep that God has entrusted to our care. Some time ago, Pastor Hsu and I decided to attempt some kind of training programme for our people. After church, we got eleven people together, four young people from the choir, and the rest elderly parishioners who were with us right from the start. At the first meeting, we were interested in finding out the sort of religious questions for which they want anwers. Right away, Tien Second Sister said: "The most important thing about Christianity is that when we die, our soul does not die. The Christian soul is immortal." The young people concurred. I was stunned. That's no Christianity. We have Easter.

This is what I mean. We need good Christian nurture, solid teaching. I can see more and more people taking an interest in religion, certainly in Christianity. But I fear that we are becoming another superstitious cult. I fear that we shall become divided again, accusing each other in front of people. I fear that we are failing to present the word of God.

12. SET APART

It is not easy for Christians from the outside world to understand this. But a long while ago, we made a decision to be a holy people, setting ourselves apart for the cause of the gospel. This means, among other things, that we will not be part of the Three Self Movement nor will we take part in public Sunday services, no matter what. I guess you can call us an underground church, the way you were met by one of us near the bus stop and brought here in a round-about way.

I have been made the Responsible Brother for a period of three years. This is my second term. To fulfil my Godgiven task, I gave up my job as an acountant, and devoted myself full-time to the care of the church. My brothers and sisters take care of my needs. We tithe. That's something we commit ourselves to. There are fourteen of us, myself included. We have enough.

As the Responsible Brother, my tasks are four, very clearly defined.

1. I pray. About two hours each day. I pray for each member of the church by name. I lift them up to God for grace and strength.

2. I study the scriptures another two to three hours. Every week I give a 45-minute to one-hour "light from the scriptures" Bible study after worship.

3. I examine the faith of the believers. At least twice a month, I am required to get together with each church member for an hour, usually two to three hours, for an examination of the heart. Here we go into matters of the soul and of the spirit. We talk and pray and struggle together. I have authority to demand submission.

4. I attend a church council meeting once a month in which I am questioned by all members of the church about my work, my spiritual state, and the affairs of the church. They can ask any question they want to about me, and I must expose myself totally in front of my brothers and

sisters. They can also make public confession if the Spirit moves them.

With regard to the worship, you have now attended one service. Brother Chang and two others are in charge. He is a water-works worker. At the service, I cease to be the Responsible Brother. Before the direct presence of God, every one is equal. After the service, I give my Bible message.

Every worship is a communion service: Christ speaking to his disciples. That is why we have a twenty-minute period of silence before communion. Any one of us can break bread. Brother Chang gives the assignment. The service is simple. we expose ourselves before God in hymns and silence, and meet him in the communion and Bible exegesis. I hope you are not offended at not being allowed to take part in communion with us. But I'm sure you shared our spirit.

Most of us in the church have our Christian roots in the indigenous Chinese Christian movement, perhaps most obviously identifiable with Teacher Wang Ming Tao. We are not Little Flock. We are not Baptist. I guess we are less sectarian than the former, and less activist and noisy than the latter.

It is true we have not been evangelizing very well. Since 1975, when we got ourselves organized again, only three have joined us, while we lost two through death and three to Hong Kong. They joined their families. It worried us but not too greatly. Christian faithfulness must come first. We have long decided not to compromise in any way in exchange for a more relaxed life. We must be faithful to God's call for holiness. "Be ye separate."

This is why we want no part of the public Sunday services. It pains me to see many of God's servants give up their principles and go the easy way. I do not question their faith, but it's the wrong setting, the wrong circumstances. It is one thing to pray and preach. And quite another thing to pray and preach under the so-called tolerance of an atheistic power. To participate in that is to participate in a clown show. There is no option for us but to separate ourselves for holiness. Times are bad. Christians must prepare for all eventualities.

With regard to the Three Self Movement, I would only say that the believer and the non-believer do not share the same yoke. Their sermons may sound evangelical, but they don't mean it. It's all a show in concert with the Religious Affairs Bureau and in pursuit of their goal of religious control.

I am not a political man. I support the People's Government as everybody does. But as a Christian, I can have no consort with atheistic communism. No Christian in close fellowship with God would or could do so without losing his soul. I know that quite a number of famous evangelical pastors are also members of the Three Self Movement Committee now. God only knows why. But God would always leave behind his faithful to bear his name. We hope we are worthy. The only important thing for a Christian is to be constantly in Christ, hidden in him, to appreciate his glory and beauty, worship him, enjoy him, and look forward to his coming in the fullness of his glory.

You ask me about the three new members. Sau Lin is twenty-six, recently married to Brother Chan. We had known of their going out together for months. Brother had been concerned about her salvation. At the time, marriage was out of the question. But Brother Chan prayed. Then one day, somehow, the Holy Spirit moved Sau Lin to seek me out. We talked for a whole afternoon. She poured out her heart, and confessed Christ on the spot. So we supported the relationship and soon they were married. Sau Lin is new to the faith. She has much to learn.

Another of the three, Tso, has been with us for two years. He's an Indonesian Chinese, stuck here permanently because he could not go back to Indonesia, and Hong Kong would not have him. He has no work, no family. His wife left him some years back. Now he depends entirely on transfers from his parents in Java. I saw him several times in a nearby park in the morning, just sitting around and reading newspapers, doing nothing. Finally I approached him, and immediately he hung on to me and told me everything. He was so lonely he had almost gone crazy. At the time, he'd simply given up. He's a skilled electrician. He could have easily got a job, but he could not bring himself to do any organized work. So we talked and I led him to

Christ. After some time, we welcomed him to our fellowship. His is one of the sad stories of our time. He had left Indonesia for China in 1962, like many Indonesian Chinese at the time. He wanted to be involved in the construction of a socialist society here. He spent two years in a technical institute, did well in both technical and political studies. He got an important maintenance job. He got married. But he was never fully accepted by his colleagues. Maybe it had to do with his having money from abroad, which automatically lifted him up above many others. Of course foreign exchange became a dirty word in the Cultural Revolution. Then his wife left him. He became depressed. He applied for a visa for Hong Kong, gave up his job, and began waiting. I hope his turn will come soon.

Lee Aunt came to us as a result of faithful prayers. She had cancer in the nose. After four months in the hospital, she was sent home to wait for the end. There was nothing more the doctors could do for her, except for a weekly prescription of a pain-killing drug which could only be obtained in the hospital clinic. She was not strong enough to take a bus. So she could not make it. One day, her neighbour, who knew I was a Christian, mentioned her to me, casually wondering "if religion could do something in that situation". I don't practise faith healing. I didn't believe or disbelieve in it. I had simply never thought about it. But at that point I felt an obligation to visit the old woman. So I went. She was in pain, crawling in bed. I tried to talk to her about Jesus, about the need for repentance. But I didn't know if she heard me. So I prayed, the only thing I could do. I visited her during the next several days. She was happy I went, but did not respond to anything I did or said. Anyway, before I left, I always prayed with her. And I remember praying for her healing. As she got better, I stopped my visits. The woman gradually disappeared from my mind. Two months later, she found her way to my home, bringing a chicken and half a dozen eggs. They were her gifts to me. She said the doctors told her she's apparently all right now. The cancer in the nose seemed to have gone. She was happy and grateful and fell on her knees before me. I was so frightened I fell on my knees too. We embraced each other. And I thanked God aloud for what he had done.

We do not worry too much about the future of our church. Our mission is to be faithful, whatever the consequences, future or no future. It is in the Lord's hands. We do not care about human judgment. Only God's judgment.

I have not thought much about it, but my hope is that the Lord will return soon, that many may come to know him before it's too late. Maybe through us, or maybe through others.

13. WHEN CAN WE HAVE A CHRISTIAN "LONG MARCH"?

I am fortunate to have a job in a tourist restaurant as a waiter. The pay is adequate. I eat well. But there is no future in it. What is the way out for me? I am not learning anything. Looking at myself honestly, I possess nothing of a useful nature. I know nothing. I have no skill. I can read, yes, and write a little, but certainly not enough to hold an office job. The other day, I picked up a magazine on electronics for beginners, and I found I could not finish the first page. I simply do not know enough to follow the instructions. I am lucky I have this restaurant job. I am thirty-three, and half of my life — the most important fifteen years of it — has been a total waste. Maybe I exaggerate. But we of the generation of the Cultural Revolution have no place in society today. And rightly so, for what can we do? Bombard the headquarters? Serve the people? No, we serve the people's dollars. China has many needs. But our generation is not the one to meet these needs. We know so little. My daughter, eight years old, is better than I in arithmetic. When my supervisor circulated a sheet asking for names of those who desire to take part in an elementary management-training course in the city, at public expense, I eagerly sent in my name. Later on, when I learned that there would be an interview, I withdrew. But I should have expected that in the first place.

My father is a very different kind of person. He's very well educated. He understands English. He can just stand up and make a speech. There is reason in his words. People respect him. He is a pastor. He got me this job. He helped out in translating many important things into English for the restaurant and hotel in the early days. So they took me in. My father must be sixty-three now. Of course, he has gone through a lot. I have gone through lot too. But his heart has not died. Mine has, if I may be frank. I am a Christian. I should not be saying things like that. It's only that my father is different.

I remember many incidents about my father.

When I was in primary one, seven years old, my father began insisting on the whole family having worship together, and he preached. There were grandma, mother, and my three older brothers. Before that we used only to say a prayer at the meal table. My father insisted that we should all be present, and he resorted to caning us if we failed to turn up. It was never a problem with me, being young and always at home. But not for my brothers, especially as father had never fixed a definite hour for the family worship. Sometimes he came home late, so naturally there was no service. One of my brothers rebelled, and was severely caned, causing mother and grandma to cry and try to stop the fight. Then father retreated to his study. I could not remember a single word of father's many home sermons. I remember, however, mother telling me that my father was anxious that we understand the word of God and that it would help us understand father and what he was doing then. I can understand that, but father was using the wrong approach. Even now when I raise with him things of those days, the old man will not talk much. He will only say: "We should forget the past. Leave it to historians." Anyway, because of the sad incident involving my brother, my father relented and thereafter decided on a fixed date for family prayers — Friday evening. When father was at a meeting, mother would stand in for him. Being a preacher, my father preached. Mother couldn't, so she told Bible stories and led us in singing and praying. I preferred mother's way. Father became increasingly busy and was seldom at home until late at night. So mother gradually took over. We memorized the scriptures and the hymns, and we prayed for father. At this point, to our shock, my elder brother declared himself an atheist. He stopped coming to the prayers, and we did not feel like a family any more. At about the same time, Aunt Tse, wife of the Methodist pastor, began joining us at the Friday prayer. Mother was happy for her company. Soon, our house was full. There must have been fifty people, mostly women of my mother's age. On Sundays, we went to church. Not to our own but to the Baptist church. Our church had been turned over to a government outfit for an exhibition hall. Sometimes father preached. Other times, he celebrated communion. Several years later, he volunteered to work in a factory, first as a worker, then as one of the manager comrades. At the same time, he became more involved with the Friday prayer service, leading it every time he was home. People loved him, loved his Bible talks. One Friday evening, over ten men came home with him. They were his comrades at work. They came to sit in on the meeting. They were very shy, insisting on sitting on the floor. I was later to learn that eventually two of them became Christians and father's best friends.

When the sparks of the Cultural Revolution began to fly, I was on fire. I felt that as a young man I had to go into the rural areas and serve my people there. My father did not stand in the way. At the next Friday meeting, he told the gathering and asked them to pray for me and my comrades. Looking back, I am glad I went away. If I had stayed on I would probably have participated in closing down the prayer meeting and in injuring my parents and other Christians when the Cultural Revolution turned against the religious and the educated.

None could escape the Cultural Revolution. It swept all across China like a tidal wave. Our hearts danced and we were full of excitement. On a grey winter morning, 43 of us set out on our "long march" of some 400 kilometres to the Green Field Mount. Our one desire was to carry the Thoughts of Chairman Mao to this remote village and kindle the sparks of revolutionary fire deep in the heart of our people. I spent the next eight years in Green Field Mount. So did most of my friends. A few died. I don't know how much good I did to the peasants. I hope I didn't do much harm. But those were wasted years for me. From 17 to 26, when I should have been in university learning something useful, I fooled around, talking about things I didn't really understand, and doing things which now seem terribly naive and irrational. I got married, only because my parents were able to send me RMB$210. Just as I came to the realization that my heart had died and saw I must resign myself to be a simple peasant in Green Field Mount with my wife, my father's letter arrived asking me if I would go home. Mother was ill. So we found our way home. It took us five days.

It turned out that mother was recovering from a mild

stroke, and was doing quite well. Father was much thinner, but vigorous. My brothers were away. We had only the big sitting room for our use in the house. Three other families had moved in and taken over the other rooms. All our books were gone, including my father's Bible and hymn books. But he had not suffered much physical pain. By the time the Red Guards processed our family, my father had already been working in the factory for a few years. They simply "demoted" him, which didn't mean anything as far as the pay was concerned. The Friday prayer service was now attended by only a few people, but it continued. My father told me:

> About a week after the Red Guards came to us, made an inventory of our possessions, took away the books and most of the furniture, five came again and demanded to be present at our Friday prayer. They were not hostile, but sounded highly sarcastic, wanting to find out at first hand this Christian superstition business. Word of their presence got around soon, but six of our group still showed up, making it eight of us plus five of them. We sat awkwardly together. I explained the situation and tried to be natural. I lighted a candle and I opened with Psalm 27:
>
> The Lord is my light and my salvation
> Whom shall I fear?
> The Lord is the strength of my life,
> Of whom shall I be afraid?
>
> Of course I would make no comments in front of these people, but I led the group through it once more line by line. The female leader of the Red Guards jeered aloud. I somehow followed my impulse to shout her down: "If you keep doing this, we can't go on." She kept her mouth shut. Then we prayed. I asked that we pray for each other. For those who were not with us. For the comfort of the Holy Spirit. Then we bowed our heads. No one spoke. Absolute silence. But I felt we were silent not because we were intimidated, though this could have been the case earlier in the opening minutes of the meeting. Now we were silent because we were praying. We somehow had decided together wordlessly that silence is our prayer in front of an enemy. We were not going to let them take the name of the Lord in vain. I personally felt the presence of the Spirit. Then it happened. The female leader suddenly burst out in hysteria. She

shouted: "Speak up, you fool. Speak up." We disregarded her. She couldn't stand it any longer. She kicked me in the thigh, grabbed my collar and pulled me up, shouting into my face: "Speak up. Pray." I felt strangely at peace. I gently wiped her tears away with my hand. She let go and walked away with her colleagues.

For the next five years, I myself was without a job, lending a hand here and there with carpentry. Our needs were minimal. The Friday prayers continued. During the height of the Cultural Revolution, my father directed that groups of no more than three meet to pray. Since 1978, we have reassembled again on Fridays. But our place can only take fifteen, so a second group began meeting on Sunday. Now we have the use of the whole house again. So we have come back to our usual Friday prayers, with worship and communion on Sunday. Father is in charge of both.

We have thirty Bibles, the full Bible, in the house. About half of the believers have their own. So we nearly have enough. It was about two years ago that the police came and asked my father to come to the police station. There were thirty old Bibles neatly stacked. So he took them home.

We have been talking about opening a church down near the marketplace right next to the New China Bookshop. The authorities seem to be sympathetic and we believe we can get help from the big city church in terms of advice on getting back the premises. So we are optimistic, although things move slowly and the hurdles are many — compensating the tenants, repair, paperwork and not least seeking out some other church workers.

I believe I am a better Christian now. I need God's presence and I know Jesus is with me. But my personal problems bother me. There is no future. Every day is the same. I have so little to look forward to. I at least have my fellow Christians to turn to, a place where I pray and sing and let God's words flow over me. But it is not just for me. There are these millions of my generation. When I think of myself, I think of them. When can we have another "long march", hard and poor, but going together, sharing things together, not just serving people's dollars? Do you know if there is really such a thing as a Christian marching song?

14. WHEN JESUS DID NOT COME AGAIN

I was almost eleven when I heard that Jesus would be coming again in three months' time. My parents, together with some hundred people, left their jobs, their homes and relatives and followed Aunt Tse Zee to a small farm on the outskirts of our town. The farm used to belong to a member of our fellowship who had turned it over to the group for the purpose of spiritual prayers. We arrived, and right away began to pray and to fast and to await Jesus' coming. The deacons set up the tents, for there were not enough rooms, boiled the water and cooked the meal. We children helped out. Simple food was available all the time and well heated; the "virgins", i.e. everyone but us, kept on praying and fasting until they fell asleep or had to eat. Most kept a ten-to-twelve-hour vigil, then slept and ate a little, while others kept the praying and singing going, pleading for Jesus' return and for mercy. On occasion, Aunt Tse Zee would ask everyone to sit and she would then give a long sermon on Jesus' coming. This went on for many weeks. Several persons collapsed, and some died. There were praises and tears, for they had returned to the bosom of the Spirit. I heard several say these people had seen glimpses of God through their prayers, and the sight was so tremendously wonderful it took away their earthly lives.

At one point, the children became unruly. Life was getting boring and we were not allowed out of the farm. So Aunt Tse Zee ordered my mother to stay away from the prayer several hours each day to teach us children in order to keep us out of trouble. So my mother told us Bible stories and taught us many things. Every day friends would come in from town and tell how the communists were tightening control of the churches and many Christians were bending their heads to them. This made us pray all the more fervently.

The three months passed. Nobody saw Jesus return. There was silence all over the farm. Everyone was bewildered. Aunt Tse Zee, who had been so serene and strong, locked herself in her room, looking very dishevelled. She came out after the night and, addressing no particular person, spoke rather incoherently. She told us that the fellowship had been found wanting in holiness and in purity of heart. So God would not come to us. Many Christians had denied God, including once-genuine believers. Therefore fulfilment had to be delayed until the number of the elect could be complete. She also confided in us that Jesus had appeared to her in her vigil, and that it seemed that Jesus had wanted to meet her at the heavenly Home rather than on earth. But she wasn't sure.

The next two or three days were spent in prayer and exhortation on meeting the coming trials. The second coming was no longer alluded to. Aunt Tse Zee and the six deacons spent a lot of time in her room, obviously discussing the fellowship's future. Then the whole group was called together to commit our lives once again to the Lord. It was announced that the group should split into two, one returning to home in the town and the other going south to join our brother fellowship. They would receive us. Aunt Tse Zee would lead the first. She said she was going home to meet Jesus. She looked serene and strong again.

Separately, we left the farm. My father sent a message to his brother in the town to send us a truck. It arrived and we drove home, together with the tents and Aunt Tse Zee. As we were about to start the engine, my father begged Aunt Tse Zee not to go home but to join the group going south. She refused.

I remember our truck being stopped as we approached the town and Aunt Tse Zee was taken away by the police. I never saw her again. My parents did, visiting her in jail. Aunt Tse Zee was charged and convicted of spreading subversive thought leading to passive resistance to the Revolution; she was therefore an anti-revolutionary. She was also convicted of causing the death of several people. I learned much later that she died in jail.

Fortunately, not much happened to the rest of us, except to an elderly woman who was headmistress of a famous Christian school. She had left her position abruptly against her pastor's advice to join us and to wait for Jesus' return.

Now she could not go back to her job and her home which was in the school compound. So the fellowship took care of her. My father returned to his family business — a spinning and weaving mill. His brother had almost given up hope. The other families soon re-established life's routine. There must have been a lot of suspicions about us, but the families of the fellowship had never had too much to do with others anyway.

With Aunt Tse Zee gone, my father became leader of the fellowship, preaching and taking care of money matters. He soon gave up his responsibility at the mill and devoted himself full-time to the fellowship. He spent a lot of time reading the scriptures. One day, during the preaching service, he asked the church if he should join a study group on Marxism with other Protestant clergymen. There was much disagreement. Finally, they settled on leaving my father to make his own decisions, with the guidance of the Holy Spirit. Tremendous changes were taking place in China and in our town. Without the guidance of the Spirit, we would perish.

My father decided to join the town's clergy to study Marxism, twice a week. Then he took to reading books intensively. He never told me what he thought. But I could sense a more relaxed father.

The good time was short-lived. Soon churches began to be taken over by the municipal authorities. Of the five Protestant churches in town, only one was left for public worship. We were encouraged to worship with other Christians. My father was agreeable, but his people refused. So we decided to worship at home. Four homes were selected, one of which was of course ours. At the first meeting, we counted over thirty people. But our home was spacious. Soon others began to join us too, including many from the Baptist and Presbyterian churches. At one time, we had more than a hundred on a Sunday.

There was nothing novel about our meetings. We began at around ten o'clock in the morning, mainly singing, scripture reading, testimonies and intercession. Then the women went off to prepare a meal of buns and noodles. When we got together again, we had our preaching service, with father giving a one-hour, sometimes a two-hour, sermon. By the time we broke off around three o'clock, the sky was already dark. The day was almost gone.

At one time, father was challenged by Brother Shen, the leader of two groups originally of the fellowship, for allowing non-believing sects to share at the Lord's Table. By non-believing sects, he meant the Presbyterians and Baptists, and the newcomers. For it used to be that while worship was open to all sincere enquirers, the Lord's Table was available only to members of the fellowship and then only after a vigorous spiritual scrutiny. My father fasted for two days and then delivered a powerful three-hour sermon in his defence. Everybody took copious notes. It began to circulate as a pamphlet. And it proved to be the beginning of a big spiritual renewal. His sermon was called "The Blood of Christ Washes Away all our Sins". I remember father flinging open his arms, earnestly demanding: "Love you one another, as God has loved us even unto death." Much much later, this pamphlet was to cost him his life in the hands of the Red Guards. (Plus the fact of our capitalist elements.) To them, I remember clearly in 1970, the blood of the revolutionary was alone redemptive. Yes, they used the same word "redemptive". But this was yet to come.

The revival came almost immediately. People at the house meeting broke down, embraced each other and openly confessed their sins. They went home and did the same to their relatives and families. Next morning, a lot of people gathered at our door, waiting to confess to my father the wrongs they had done him. They stayed and prayed. My father urged them to return to their work. He told them it was not pleasing to the Spirit that Christians abandon their work and responsibility. If we must pray, let us pray in the privacy of our homes. Despite his caution, many people stayed to pray. My father had personally to embrace each one, bring him to his feet and gently escort him out into the care of waiting brothers and sisters who would take him home.

The authorities were alarmed. They sent for my father. Nothing happened to him. But some time later, he returned to his job in the mill and remained there until the time of the Red Guards. Our meetings continued, but father was no longer willing to take leadership. He would not preach. With great reluctance, he explained that he had found too much of the human element in his own preaching, and that we all must learn to depend on God rather than on human individuals. I believe he was seeking a much quieter and more common and ordinary faith.

During this period we wrote a number of hymns. One of them is as follows:

Angels on high, strengthen me,
Walk us through this Dragon Hill.
This land toss and turn and roar;
Calm its brave heart, still our fear.

What happened to us in the late 60s was simply indescribable. As the largest and best-organized Christian group in town, we were the first under attack. The local brigade teamed up with a provincial contingent and broke into our meeting, confiscated all our Bibles, hymn books and gospel posters and took my father and two others away. It was not unexpected, except that eight other church workers who had been inactive for some time were also rounded up. Several days later, we were told to line up in the street, and watched father, our brothers and sisters, several senior party officials, and ten or twelve teachers forced to take part in a mock parade. My father died soon after the experience. He was seventy-nine.

Our prayer meetings could not go on. Nobody would show up. We could not even be seen greeting each other in the streets.

Around about 1975 or 1976, Christians were meeting in homes again. Pastor Chung of what used to be the Presbyterian Church reappeared and word soon circulated of Christians meeting with him. We took heart and soon revived our meeting. Pastor Chung paid us a visit and gave us his New Testament. We held hands and prayed aloud, thanking the Lord for his word.

There is as yet no public worship in our town. Pastor Chung is working on it. We had made a number of enquiries about getting back part of our fellowship property but to no avail. As of now, there are over fifty people in our service, about half over sixty, the rest young people in their teens and twenties. We have many needs. But the main thing is we have survived and have not dishonoured the name of Jesus.

APPENDIX

AN OPEN LETTER TO BROTHERS AND SISTERS IN CHRIST OF ALL CHINA FROM THE STANDING COMMITTEE OF THE CHRISTIAN MOVEMENT FOR SELF-GOVERNMENT, SELF-SUPPORT, AND SELF-PROPAGATION

The "Open Letter" was adopted at an enlarged meeting of the standing committee of the Three-self Patriotic Movement of the Protestant Churches, which was held in Shanghai from February 25 to March 1, 1980. Twenty-four standing committee members from sixteen provinces and municipalities as well as thirteen local church leaders attended the meeting. The translation of this letter came from China.

Dear brothers and sisters in Christ in all parts of China:

First of all we greet you in the name of Christ. We cannot but thank God for being able to address you once again openly in this matter. His rod and his staff were never far from us as we moved through the valley of the shadow of death. His promise to Joshua, "I will always be with you; I will never abandon you" (Jos. 1:5), has been actualized in our midst these years.

Today, through this letter, let us speak to you about things of our common concern.

For the first time in over ten years the Standing Committee of our national Three-Self movement met in Shanghai during the last week. As we listened to colleagues' reports on church conditions in different parts of China, we felt specially close to our brothers and sisters in the whole household of God and prayed with special fervency for God's blessing on you.

In closing our meeting today we are struck by the fact that the meeting has been so similar to the one in Jerusalem as recorded in Acts 15. We did not have a set agenda. We just let the Holy Spirit guide us as we entered into all subjects of deep concern to us.

Although in the recent past the policy of religious freedom was trespassed upon by the Lin Piao and the "gang of four" cliques, and although many of our clergy and leaders of Three-Self organizations had to suffer all sorts of persecution alongside leading cadres of religious affairs bureaus and of other governmental organs, as well as many intellectuals, yet it heartens us to learn that large numbers of Christians all over China have persisted in their faith, that their service, prayer, and waiting before God has not ceased and that they have witnessed well in places where they work. We have seen that the church has not let her light to be put out but has gone through trials and been strengthened, and that our witness to Christ also has not been dimmed but has in quietude borne fruit. All these years we have firmly believed that the correct line of the Communist Party would return to New China. We have firmly believed that the policy of religious freedom laid down by Chairman Mao and Premier Chou En-Lai was correct and could not be permanently abrogated by anybody. We have firmly believed that the Chinese Church, through the Three-Self movement, would become cleansed and fair, an abode for the Lord. We have firmly believed that upheavals would pass and stability would be restored, bringing a bright prospect for New China. And we have firmly believed that we Christians who cherish a love both for our motherland and for our religious faith would surely be able to work alongside the rest of our Chinese people and make our contributions to our motherland.

Brothers and sisters, today China has indeed returned to the correct orientation. As we met and listened to all the encouraging reports summarized above, we were greatly moved and inspired by Christian examples. They turned our hearts to thanksgiving. Our faith in the gospel of Christ became strengthened. We are resolved more than ever to unite and do the work entrusted us by God and by fellow-Christians of the whole country, so that what we have firmly believed can all be turned into facts.

We need to develop and strengthen further our movement.

The Three-Self patriotic movement has achieved a great

deal in the course of the last thirty years. As a result of this movement more and more Chinese Christians have come to cherish our motherland. There is a heightened sense of national pride on our part as Chinese and we are now much closer to the people of China in our thinking and standing. As a result of this movement Chinese Christianity is no longer a tool exploited by imperialism or by other reactionary forces. It is now basically a religion adhered to by Chinese citizens. Also as a result of this movement more and more of our Chinese people and cadres have changed their attitude towards Christianity. It is no longer a foreign religion encouraging its adherents to be unpatriotic but is a religion governed, supported, and nurtured by Chinese Christians ourselves. These are all very important changes from the perspective of Christian witness in China during the long, coming historical period. And we could not possibly see these changes had there not been the initiation of this movement by the late Mr. Y. T. Wu and other faithful servants of God.

Today, we fellow-Christians all over China are rebuilding our Temple with the same zeal as that of the Old Testament prophets Haggai, Zechariah, and Zerubbabel. We believe that under the guidance of the eternal God our Father the glory of the latter Temple will be greater than of the former.

We gave heed to the yearning of our brothers and sisters in all parts of our country for the publication of our own Bible and have decided to hasten this work.

We gave heed to the big demand for other Christian publications and have decided to resume the work of preparing such personnel.

There is a big need for well-trained clergy and church workers and we have decided to resume the work of preparing such personnel.

In some parts of China the policy of religious freedom has not been very well implemented and we want to do our best to assist our government and other related bodies in putting the policy into effect.

We need to strengthen our relations with Christian communities everywhere, help solve their existing problems, and help Christians in their endeavours to glorify God and bring benefit to men and women.

We also need to help elevate the consciousness of our constituencies so that all Christians in China will love our motherland, adhere to state laws and prevent anyone with ulterior motives from using Christianity as a cover for activities detrimental to social order, endangering our people and defaming our church.

In short, we need greatly to strengthen the pastoral work of our Christian communities. This is an urgent task which calls for our deep commitment and leads us in a most concerted way to see the necessity of the formation of a Christian national structure. After earnest prayer and long deliberation we have decided to proceed with the preparatory work for this organization. This organization aims at giving the necessary pastoral help to Christians and Christian communities across China. It is above all a serving agency. In any question that has to do with our faith our principle is to practice mutual respect and not to interfere with or to make uniform our beliefs.

The relation between this new national structure and the Three-Self organization is going to be like that between the two hands of a body. There will be no question of one giving and the other accepting any leadership. The formation of the new body does not at all imply the winding up of the work of the Three-Self movement and its organizations. Rather the latter work is to be carried forth more extensively and deeply. We need to continue to uphold the banner of the motherland and give encouragement to Christians to unite with the rest of the Chinese people, contribute to the task of the four modernizations, safeguard the stability and unity of our country, and oppose aggression and defend world peace. We need to continue to uphold the banner of national independence, of self-government, self-support, and self-propagation, promote Three-Self reeducation among our Christians, raise further the sense of national self-respect, defend the fruits of the Three-Self movement, enhance the love of the brethren and the practice of mutual respect in matters of Christian faith which have become the heritages of our movement, and guard against the divisive tactic of those trying to undermine the movement.

We are aware that in churches abroad there is a small number of people still hostile to New China today. They attack our principled stand on Three-Self and put their hands into our church life in the name of "evangelism" and "research." Regardless of the color of their skin, they are trying in reality to push Chinese Christianity back to the colonial past and earn for it again the onus of a foreign religion taking its stand against the Chinese people. We hope that these individuals would not receive the support of the other Christians abroad and their leaders. We are sure their pursuits will not bear good fruit in the long run.

As to those Christians abroad who assume an attitude of equality towards us and respect our principled stand on independence and self-government, we are ready to enter into friendly relations and fellowship with them.

In order to turn our intentions into facts, we have decided to call a national Christian conference in the near future in which, aside from the discussion of other important questions, we will produce the new national committee of the Three-Self movement and go into the question of the formation of the Christian national organization. These are questions which concern every Christian and we request you to put the conference in your prayers. If you have any opinion regarding our Christian work in China today, please write to us at 169 Yuen Ming Yuen Road, Shanghai, so that we can take it into consideration at an early stage.

As we meet we remember with love our brothers and sisters in Taiwan and sincerely hope for the return of Taiwan to the bosom of our motherland within this new decade. Then we will be able to join together in rendering our common worship to the One Lord. Let all our fellow-Christians pray and work for the dawn of that day.

In spite of the fact that we are unworthy servants of Christ, let us pray that, in God's blessing, a Chinese Church befitting the new countenance of our motherland will soon arise on the beloved soil of China.